Do You Know Where You Are Going?

My wife Mary and me, with our son, Jeremy

Do You Know
Where You Are Going?

*One Man's Story of September 11
and the Saving Grace of Jesus Christ*

Sujo John

*Man is destined to die once,
and after that to face judgment*

—Hebrews 9:27

Lantern Books • New York
A Division of Booklight Inc.

2002
Lantern Books
One Union Square West, Suite 201
New York, NY 10003

Copyright © Sujo John 2002

Printed in the United States of America

Library of Congress Cataloging-in-Publication Data

John, Sujo.
  Do you know where you are going? : one man's story of September 11 and the saving grace of Jesus Christ / Sujo John.
    p. cm.
  ISBN 1-59056-039-6 (alk. paper)
  1. John, Sujo. 2. Christian biography—United States. 3. September 11 Terrorist Attacks, 2001. I. Title.
  BR1725.J55 A3 2002
  277.3'083'092—dc21

                                                          2002008900

*This book is dedicated
to my beautiful wife, Mary,
and our bundle of joy, Jeremy*

❦ Table of Contents

Acknowledgments 🌓

I WOULD LIKE to acknowledge and thank deeply the following: My father and mother, who raised me in the love of the Lord and who have always been there for me.

My grandmother, whose prayer life has been the biggest strength of my life.

Rev. Drs. Mark and Huldah Buntain, for leaving such an important mark on my life. I am truly honored that Huldah Buntain chose to write the foreword to this book.

My pastor, Reverend Don James of Bethany Church, Wyckoff, New Jersey, and his wife Donna, who gave Mary and me direction and timely counsel when I suddenly found myself in an evangelistic ministry; and to the many pastors in the many cities that I have visited who have encouraged me to press on with my message.

The many friends and well-wishers who have come up to me at my services encouraging me to put my thoughts in a book. If it had not been for your confidence in my message, this book would only have been a dream.

All of you that have been praying for us, your prayers have been our support system.

The many who have touched my life in a direct or indirect way: my Sunday School teachers, pastors, and all my friends who believed in me.

Martin Rowe and Lantern Books, who had faith in this first-time author and who helped me express my thoughts through this book. Without Lantern this book would not have happened.

Above all, all glory and praise to Lord Jesus Christ, the author and finisher of my faith, the Master Carpenter, who is still working on my life.

Foreword 🌿

I COUNT IT a privilege to write the foreword to this wonderful book by Sujo John, whom I have known from childhood. Sujo never settled for an average life. In this book he shares his story of growing up in Calcutta, India, and how he was able to look beyond the tragedy of human suffering and let God use his life.

If your life is programmed to be negative, to disbelieve and be skeptical, your life can be changed. What God did for Sujo He can do for you by transforming the negatives of your life into positives.

It all happened one night in our church in Calcutta, after a message my late husband, Rev. (Dr.) Mark Buntain, spoke to a group of teenagers. Many came forward to the altar that evening, and Sujo was one of them. He was deeply touched and felt the message was just for him. At the altar while praying, Pastor Buntain laid his hand on Sujo's head and spoke these words: "God is going to change the destiny of your life and is going to use you to bless millions of people." Little did Sujo realize that night that this prophecy would become a reality. From that day his life was changed. He became a leader among our young people, willing and ready to work for the Lord whether the task was large or small.

Sujo has wonderful, godly parents who were a great influence in his life. Their strong faith after the death of Sujo's sister was a pillar of strength in his life. I know it was in answer to their prayers that the Lord brought a beautiful Christian Indian girl to Calcutta. This young lady had been raised from a young age in the United States and her parents were friends of Sujo's parents. In this book you will read a miraculous love story and of a marriage certainly ordained by God. It will be an encouragement to every young person to know what God can to do for those who are committed and dedicated to him.

After coming to the United States Sujo often became discouraged, as he felt that he was not doing as much for God as he had done in India, where the need was great. However, so often God works in mysterious ways, which are not on our timetable but are definitely on His. This became a reality on September 11, 2001, an ordinary day that turned into a most extraordinary one in Sujo's life.

That day, thousands of miles away in Calcutta, Sujo's parents turned on CNN when they came home from work (Calcutta being ahead of New York by nine and a half hours). They could not believe what they saw and immediately dropped to their knees in prayer. Their son and daughter-in-law worked at the World Trade Center. Relatives and friends hearing the news soon joined them. Across the world their prayers reached heaven and God worked one of the greatest miracles for Sujo and Mary, a story you will not want to stop reading and one you will never forget.

I can never thank God sufficiently for the way He is using Sujo's testimony week after week as he speaks to large audiences impacting and changing the destiny of so many lives. Often in Calcutta I read the words on my husband's grave—"He lives on in the lives he touched." How true this has been in Sujo's life and also in the lives of many others in Calcutta.

As you read these pages you will find the formula to redirect your life to spiritual fulfillment and a road map for your life so that you, too, may know where you are going.

Rev (Dr.) Huldah Buntain is Senior Pastor Emeritus and President of the Mark Buntain Memorial Assemblies of God Church in Calcutta, India.

Introduction 🌿

A T 8:04 A.M. on September 11, 2001, I was in my office on the eighty-first floor of the World Trade Center writing an email to a friend about the lack of purpose in my life. I felt I had a mission, but that I hadn't been fulfilling it in recent days. I had just come from India, was married to a beautiful woman, and had a dream job, working in a famous building that overlooked the Statue of Liberty. Yet something was missing.

Forty minutes later, I was laying flat on my stomach, flame and debris all around me, and I thought I was going to die. Two hijacked planes had slammed into the Twin Towers of the World Trade Center, causing the death of thousands of people and turning the world upside down. What happened that day—the scenes of death and terror, huddles of bodies and horrifying explosions, as well as moments of great courage and transforming faith—will stay with me forever. They form the heart of this book. You can read about what happened that day in Chapter Four.

Yet this book aims to tell something more than what happened to me and my wife and the lessons I drew from my experiences. My goal is to tell much more than a story about a tragedy. This book is a message of hope. It contains a bigger question with a larger answer than a simple account of the terrible events of that day can account for. This question is the most profound question we can ask ourselves: When we are faced with death, do we know where we are going? The question, as I discovered on September 11, could not be more pressing or the answer more profoundly important. This book challenges you, the reader, to ask yourself that question and to be honest about the answer.

I am a practicing Christian who has been blessed throughout his life with many opportunities to experience the saving grace of Jesus Christ. Yet it has not been easy. I was born in Calcutta, India, and grew up in a loving Christian home. However, I was confronted on a daily basis with the enormous suffering of human beings as I moved among some of the world's poorest people. I talk about this and the good work being done by Christian churches in Calcutta in Chapter One. In Chapter Two, I discuss another traumatic experience that shook my faith in God deeply—the loss to leukemia of my beloved sister Elizabeth, whom my family nicknamed Sheba. Yet in this period of doubt and difficulty, I was touched by the transforming experience of knowing two holy people—Mark Buntain and Mother Teresa—who offered me a glimpse of true leadership and the Christ-like life.

In Chapter Three I write about my marriage and how I came to the United States, about what America meant to me and how excited I was to find a job in the World Trade Center. In Chapter Four, I relate the events of September 11—when the planes struck, how we escaped, how I had just set foot outside the building when the tower above me collapsed, and my desperate search for Mary, my wife. I talk about how my faith was challenged in a way it had never been before and how I experienced the peace of Jesus Christ in my heart. In Chapters Five, Six, Seven, and in the conclusion, I examine the question, "Do you know where you are going?," describe what it means to be born again and live a Christ-like life, and offer a challenge to all those who experience the joy and abundance of welcoming Jesus Christ into their heart.

My message is a simple one. We spend so much of our time and energy in preparing for our future in this life, a life that is short and can be taken from us at any moment. Should we not spend much more of our energies in preparing for the next life, which is eternal and from which there is no turning back? In the United States, we expend enormous resources on saving individual lives—and this is good. But how many more resources and time should we expend on trying to save the souls of people for the life to come?

For me, Christianity is not so much a religion as a walk with God, an attempt to live a Christ-like life, and to work as much as possible to bring about God's Kingdom here on earth. September 11 taught me that life is so precious that we cannot waste a moment in not spreading the Good News of Jesus' saving grace or challenging ourselves to make sure that when we are face to face with death, as many of us were on September 11, we know where we are going.

* * *

As I mentioned at the beginning of this introduction, since September 11, my life has changed enormously. Whereas I was a stranger in the United States when I arrived, now people all over the world have heard of me and know my story. I am blessed by the hundreds of people who are praying for me and my family, encouraging me to go on with what I am doing. If it had not been for them and the strength given to me by God, I would have stopped traveling, since I now have a child and the traveling takes me away from my family. But every week, when I travel, people come up to me and tell me that my family and I are in their thoughts and they are standing behind us. Every time I preach, I realize that I am covered with the prayers of many. That is truly a blessing from God.

Before September 11, I had never really thought of my own death, even though my sister had died and I had seen so many people suffering sickness on the streets of Calcutta. Now, even though I am only twenty-seven years old, I think of death every day. Now, every morning, I realize that life is a free gift. There are many who got out of their beds that morning of September 11 and never saw another dawn. The Bible says, "As for man, his days are like grass, he flourishes like a flower of the field; the wind blows over it and it is gone, and its place remembers it no more" (Psalm 103:15–16). I am grateful for the fact that I am alive, and that I am blessed with a wife and a son, and that they are thriving. I am grateful for each new day that God in His mercy has given me, because I realize that everything that you value or hold precious, everything you treasure, could be taken away in a moment. It is good to have dreams, make plans, and look to the future. But we must always keep in mind that they can all vanish. I now realize the importance and value of life and the pain that comes from losing your loved ones. It has made me more compassionate, and I am deeply grateful for that.

Since September 11, my all too human fear of death—a fear that recurs even if you trust in your destiny—has lessened. I now realize that no matter how long I want to live, death is going to catch up with me one day. Thus, although the death of others pains me, I try and keep in mind the knowledge that they have simply gone ahead of me to a place to which I will go shortly.

Since September 11, I have not only been able to visit many parts of the United States, but I have been inspired by people of faith all across this great nation. The Christian historian Patrick Henry said: "It can not be emphasized too strongly or too often that this great nation was founded not be religionists, but by Christians: Not on religions but on the Gospel of Jesus Christ. For this very reason peoples of other faiths have been afforded asylum, prosperity, and freedom of worship here." In other words, the Founding Fathers founded this country on nothing more nor less than Jesus Christ. I have seen evidence of this on the West Coast, the East Coast, in the North and South: a network of Christians who love the Lord. We might be divided into denominations, but I have seen an enormous amount of unity in the Kingdom of God. Every person is crying out to that one God as Jesus Christ, and their prayers are being heard.

I have also seen a lot of young people all across the country on fire for God and wanting to be used in the Kingdom of God. They are not qualified in the way that the world qualifies people, with theological degrees or pulpits to declaim from, but they have something that is more important—the heart to be used by God. And God is honoring their faith and their love. If you want to be used in the Kingdom of God, as I have discovered, you do not have to be superbly talented. God is not looking for people who have a lot of resources or people who look good. God is looking for someone who has a heart and who will be available for Him. Our availability and sincerity of heart could make every one of us a world-changer. God blesses that person, so that the more you have a need for God, the bigger is the opportunity for God to use you. This book is written by one of those people whom God has blessed.

Across this land, young people are rising up. "We are going to say 'no' to the temptations of the world," is the cry. "We are going to live a Christ-like life." When I see these young people, the future of America, I am blessed, because I know that this is a country based on God, and we have a future where the coming generations are not turning away from God but are instead rooted in the Lord.

In my travels throughout North America since September 11, I have also seen how deeply people have been touched by the attacks. Young children have come to me and told me that they have not been able to sleep at night because of the images that haunt their minds. People throughout the United States have been feeling vulnerable and acknowledging how short our lives are. We are coming to terms with the reality that we cannot be protected from everything and that there is evil in the world. What makes me feel blessed is that, amidst this fear and uncertainty, I am able to offer a message of hope. "No one knows what is going to happen tomorrow," I say. "But I know one thing. If you place your hearts and your lives with the Lord, you are going to have that peace." And I invite everyone to have the peace that only God can give.

Even as I have been blessed by God to be able to touch millions of people with the message of Jesus through magazines and newspapers, radio and television, the Internet, and public events, I am hungry to reach still more. This is why I felt it was important to write this book. There are more people who need to hear the Good News. I believe that the hungrier I am, the more God will pour out His anointing on my life. And without God's anointing, I am nothing. When I go on stage or stand up in church every weekend to preach, I pray to God that He will hide me behind the cross, because I am worried that people's expectations of me will be too high or different from what I can offer. This is why I constantly seek a fresh anointing from God, so that people who come to hear me will not hear from Sujo John but from God. If I have been successful, it is a testament to God speaking through me and laying His message on my lips.

I want you who read this book to connect with Jesus, if you have not before. To you who at some point in your life gave your heart to God but were distracted by relationships or habits or disappointments, even, perhaps, by disagreements with the church, I also extend that invitation. For you who once had God in your hearts, God has given you an opportunity through reading this book to connect again with the body of Christ and with God. Come back to the first love you had for God; rekindle the flame.

My prayer is that when you read this book or when you have heard me speak you take upon you the burden for your community around you. If you could speak to two or three people about what you have read here and ask them to receive God's peace, and they could in turn do the same for two or three more, and each of those people shared the message with two or three more, then the multiplication effect is greater than any one individual could have achieved alone. In this way also we create righteous communities, zealous for the Lord. Once more, you do not have to be talented in the way the world judges talent. God wants to use you. You simply need to be open to Him. And keep praying. For there are many who use the word of God and give up, because nothing seems to change. My advice is the same as my mentor and spiritual guide Mark Buntain taught me many years ago: Never give up, but press on. God has a plan for you, and it will come to fruition.

The timing of God is something we will never understand. All we can do is to be faithful in what we are seeking and keep pressing on. In the Bible we read about Jacob wrestling with the angel of God, saying, "I will not let you go unless you bless me" (Genesis 32:26). This is how we should be with God. We should ask God, "God, use me. I want Your presence. I want Your fire in my life."

What the people of the United States went through on September 11 was a tragedy, but every human being goes through tragedies in his or her life. No tragedy is bigger to an individual than his or her own, and somebody else's tragedy is no more important or meaningful than your own. Whatever tragedy you are going through, you can call upon the name of the Lord and have an answer in Him. If you feel desperate, where every avenue of escape seems blocked and you have no more strength to fight, then know that there are answers to your problems in heaven. If you put your trust in God, and have faith like a mustard seed (Matthew 17:20), God is going to do the work of healing in your life and open up paths you thought were blocked. As Jesus says, "Ask and it will be given to you; seek and you will find; knock and the door will be opened to you" (Matthew 7:7). He has blessed us, and all you have to do is to claim those blessings.

I wish to end my introduction to this book with a word of thanks. The thanks extend out of my continually deepening connection to North America, and the United States in particular. Although I have not been physically in the United States for very long, I feel as though I know America. I am a product of the work of North American evangelists who risked everything and came to India. My church's work of helping the poor and spreading the Gospel in Calcutta and elsewhere throughout northeast India, which is the subject of the first chapter, would not be possible without the generosity and love of people throughout North America, pledging their money and their prayers to us.

In several of my talks, people have come up to me when I have finished talking and told me of the role their church played in supporting our work and the work of churches like ours. They tell me that it is such an encouragement for them to see someone from the "field" coming back and preaching the Gospel to people in the United States. It is a blessing, they say, that things have come full circle, and that an Indian who was evangelized by North Americans is coming to North America to evangelize in his turn. I share their sense of blessing. Being able to share the Good News and my sense of God's love in my life with people who have done so much to improve the conditions of individuals in my home country is my small way of thanking them for their work. This book is both a testament to them and my gift of thanks, and I hope it will be taken as such.

1 🌿
Calcutta

ALTHOUGH I WAS raised in Calcutta, a city of twenty million people on the eastern seaboard of India in the state of West Bengal, I was born into the Kaiyooril family in the province of Kerala, the ancestral home of my parents John and Susy, on the western coast of the southern tip of India. Because of its position as the gateway to India across the Indian Ocean from the Middle East, Europe, and Africa, for many Kerala has been the entryway to the Indian subcontinent. For centuries merchants traded spices and jewelry, and with them they also brought new ideas. One of those ideas was Christianity, which St. Thomas, the disciple of Christ, is reputed to have brought to Kerala in the first century.

Although Malayalees (which is what the people of Kerala call themselves) spread the Good News throughout the entire Indian subcontinent, leaving Christian communities in many places, the largest concentration of Christians in India remains in Kerala. Christians number only a little over two percent of India's one billion people, and there is unfortunately a strong negative stereotype of Christians in Indian popular culture. Indian movies often portray Christians—whom they characterize through their names and through the wearing of crosses and other religious symbols— as drug dealers or gangsters. The vast majority of Christians of course are neither drug dealers nor gangsters, but, sadly, some are not practicing their faith and are only nominally Christian. As I suggest later on in this book, Christianity is more than having a Christian name. It is about having a personal relationship with Jesus Christ. For those of us who attempt on a daily basis to walk the Lord's path, it is not easy being a Christian—either in India or anywhere else. False depictions, however, make it even harder.

In the last few years there have been incidents of mobs burning churches and killing Christian missionaries—supposedly because they are forcibly converting people to Christianity. A great deal of investigation and research has shown this not to be true. What has happened is that Christian missionaries have been entering villages and bringing about social change and reform. They have brought schools and roads and clean drinking water to villages where there were none before. Through education, some of the children of the poor and their parents, who were often servants or bondsmen of the upper castes, have become followers of Christ, because they have been educated about their rights and have rejected the caste system of their own accord. This phenomenon has led to the persecution of Christians, although Christians do not use their schools in India to proselytize about Christianity or to denigrate Hinduism or the caste system. All Christians have proclaimed is that in Christ everyone is equal and that there is no caste system. As St. Paul says, "There is neither Jew nor Greek, slave nor free, male nor female, for you are all one in Christ Jesus" (Galatians 3:28). Many who have struggled for hundreds and even thousands of years to improve their situation because of their low-caste status have embraced the real freedom that Christ offers.

My family has been Christian for as long as we have family records. My father, John, is a civil engineer, who, when I was three or four years old, left for the Middle East, where he spent many years working in Saudi Arabia, Kuwait, Bahrain, and Iraq. He finally returned just before the Gulf War and began to work for the church our family belonged to as an advisor on church construction throughout India. Although my mother and sister and I missed my father greatly, his work enabled us to have sufficient money and resources at home to live a good life. My mother currently works for a government steel company. While my parents are both inspiring sources of holiness for me, it was my grandmother, Aleyamma, who had the biggest influence on me as I was growing up. It was her influence that most fully formed the ideal of the Christ-like life to which I still aspire.

A Young Widow

My grandmother was widowed when she was only in her early thirties, after her husband died of illness. Although she had little money with which to raise her children, other family members helped her bring up my father and his brother and sister. Her response to this intense suffering was to start praying intensively to God to bless her children and to root them in the Christian faith, and when I was young, my grandmother's constant prayer and concern were to see my sister and me rooted in the faith of God. She would instill in me the importance of praying every night, reading the Bible, and being part of a church fellowship. In spite of her early loss, and because of her deep prayer life, my grandmother remained humble and faithful. Indeed, because the true spirit of Jesus was in her, no one argued with her or had a bad word to say about her.

My grandmother would always talk about how God had provided faithfully for her and for her children. And, as I grew up, I realized that one of the main reasons why God had blessed our family with sufficient resources to live a comfortable life was my grandmother's prayers. It was an inspiration to see her love for God and her nightly conversations with Him. Even today, my grandmother will pray for hours on end. If she meets someone who is involved in the church and they ask her to pray for them or someone else, she will pray for that person for as long as she is able. Over the years, she has prayed for thousands of people from all over the community. The community in turn knows that my grandmother is a prayerful woman who has led an exemplary Christian life, and that the fruits of the Holy Spirit in her life are the evidence.

The Lighthouse in the City

Growing up in Calcutta presented problems that are not unique to a large city in the developing world—indeed, not unique to any large city anywhere—but are intensified in India because of the sheer numbers of people. Simply walking through the streets of Calcutta is hard because you cannot avoid bumping into people. And this problem increases every day as the population of this lively, teeming city is swelled every morning when hundreds of thousands of people commute from the suburbs into the city to work.

For many thousands of people in Calcutta, however, there are no jobs to go to and no homes to come back to. Many thousands live and beg on the streets of Calcutta, a situation that, while desperate, is perhaps not as bad today as it was when I was growing up in the 1970s and 1980s. In those days, when you walked out of your house, you would be confronted by the sight of whole families living on the streets without food, or living in little shanties or shacks on the streets or by the railroad tracks. Inside one of these shacks you might find a single room where a mother and father would live and sleep on a wooden board, under which their seven, eight, and sometimes nine children would also live and sleep. Conditions were particularly acute during the monsoon season, when thousands of people would become susceptible to dysentery, malaria, and leprosy as the rains came.

Although, as I have said, conditions have improved for the poor, there are still a great many destitute persons in India's major cities, and the conditions in which they live are still very difficult. Calcutta has grown as the population of India has grown—a situation exacerbated by the increase in traffic throughout the city. The streets, which were created by the British to support trams and the occasional car, are now filled with two-wheeled scooters or three-wheeled bicycles, two-cylinder mopeds, trucks, and many cars, as well as trams and pedestrians. The presence of two-wheelers, trucks, and cars has substantially decreased the quality of the air in the city, so that life has become even more hazardous to the health of those on the street.

The relationship between the street dwellers and the other citizens of Calcutta is a complex one. While some see the street dwellers as a nuisance, and every now and again the police come and move them from one location to another, there are many organizations that provide assistance to the poor and seek to improve their lives. One of the organizations that is committed to helping those most in need has been the church to which my family belongs—the Mark Buntain Memorial Assemblies of God

Church. When I refer to the church throughout this book it is this church that I mean.

For many years the Mark Buntain Memorial Assemblies of God Church has stood out in Calcutta. Indeed, the church on Park Street, which is right in the heart of the city, where it can most easily serve the poor and suffering who surround it, is called the Lighthouse in the City, because it is a beacon of hope for so many. When it was established in the 1950s, the church was the first to be built in Calcutta in a century; and it is a testament to its success that, while the Christian population in Calcutta is falling, our church continues to grow.

Calcutta was never an easy place in which to evangelize, let alone build a church. In the early part of the twentieth century, Calcutta used to be called the preachers' graveyard. Preachers would come full of the zeal of the Lord, and because of malaria or cholera or other diseases they died, or lost loved ones, or went home. Yet some missionaries and preachers stayed, and two of those were Mark and Huldah Buntain. The Buntains came from Canada in 1954 after preaching for many years throughout North America, where they had become very popular evangelists. Initially, Mark Buntain had felt called to go to China, but he ended up in India, where he began his evangelical mission in a tent. With the help of a local doctor, Mark Buntain started offering basic medical services through a clinic. (In the 1970s, the church built a 175-bed hospital that currently serves both rich and poor alike.) More and more people came to the tent, and he was obliged to build a church. This original church was in Royd Street, and it has a special place in my heart as well as the hearts of many others, because it was in the prayer room in the church that I and others spent some of our most profound moments with God.

Mark Buntain died in 1989, and the church moved to much bigger facilities on Park Street. Huldah Buntain, who is in her seventies, continues to shuttle between India and North America, traveling across the United States trying to raise support for the church and its work in India. The church now has over 1,600 people on its payroll. While we conduct services in eight languages—Hindi, English (which is the service I go to), Malayalam (my mother tongue), Bengali, Tamil, Oriya, Telagu, and Nepali—we nonetheless all worship one God. In addition, our church feeds 18,000 people a day at feeding stations around Calcutta. We have people cooking all through the night so that others can be served the next morning. Our meals are big enough that they can keep people feeling fed through the entire day—often they are the only meals people will eat that day.

Our church sponsors 15,000 students a month, as well as providing some social services. The Buntains, like many Christians, including me, believed that you cannot preach the Gospel to someone who has no food to eat or clothes to wear. The Gospel is a message of love and compassion. God has blessed us so that we can not only receive the message of Jesus but also share what He has given us. In the Kingdom of God, the rules of finance are very different from the world's: The more you give toward the work of God, the more you create an opportunity for God to bless you. If you presented this plan to the financial brokers at the New York Stock Exchange, they would think it a very odd principle. But the heavenly plan is about giving what God has given you, and doing it with a cheerful heart. If you give with a cheerful heart and without a sense of your own self-worth, then God will bless you abundantly. This is why you cannot preach the Gospel of love and compassion to people who do not have anything. How can you walk up to them wearing a nice suit and talk about how God is going to take care of the situation when the person you are addressing has nothing to wear? In this way, the church provides some basic help to the people, and through our service attempts to show that we love the Lord and all are one in Him.

The church has always relied on the support of its congregation and the congregations of the Assemblies of God throughout North America, especially in the United States. One story that illustrates American generosity was shared in a church by the famous contemporary Christian singer and partner of our church Ray Boltz. He told me that one Sunday he was singing to help support our church in one of the churches in North America when a little boy, whose birthday it was, came to the altar. The little boy had heard Ray's stories about the children in India going without food and how a few cents would make a huge difference in their lives, and he approached Ray with the couple of dollars he had received as a birthday present. "This is what I got for my birthday," he said, thrusting our his hand with the two dollars in it. "How many will this feed?"

This is an example of the kind of commitment our church has had from people who have been our partners in the work of God throughout North America, Europe, and other parts of the world. Our church believes in tithing, which means that ten percent of your income is God's and should be given to charity. Even so, people are commanded to give more cheerfully, and they do. As Jesus says, "When you give to the needy, do not let your left hand know what your right hand is doing" (Matthew 6:3).

In addition to helping those less fortunate than ourselves, our church is responsible for spreading the Gospel of Christ among the 230 million people who live in eleven states in northeast India. Consequently, our church has established churches and food programs and small clinics in Bihar, Orissa, Arunachal Pradesh,

Nagaland, Manipur, Meghalaya, Tripura, Mizoram, Jharkhand, West Bengal, and Sikkim. This is where our church is reaching out, setting up schools in the smallest villages and bringing the Good News to places where, literally, no one has ever heard the name of Jesus Christ. The church has two large schools in Calcutta, which teach from first through twelfth grades and provide training and apprenticeships in carpentry, electronics, tailoring, and technical work for those who are not going to complete the academic work. There is also a nursing school to help staff the church's hospitals and clinics.

In the church's primary schools, reading, writing, and arithmetic are taught and free food and clothing provided for children, which is a big incentive for parents to bring their children to be educated. In some locations, there is a day care center where the church brings in a doctor once a week. There is also a program unit from a hospital in Calcutta where people can go and volunteer. The church also runs inoculation programs and eye-operation camps, and has been working among the sex workers of Calcutta, giving them shelter and trying to provide something for their children, so their daughters will not have to follow their mothers into the sex work business.

Our church also has a Bible college where young men and women are trained. They come from different parts of India and a few other neighboring countries, especially from the eight states where our church is active. They enroll at Bible college, get trained, and bring the Gospel into the villages. We run different courses through high school and up to a bachelor's degree in theology, and have a large number of mission schools where short-term missions programs are taught in satellite Bible colleges. There are fifty to sixty graduates every year. A memory that has stuck with me until today is an encounter with one young man who told me he had illegally walked across the border from Burma just to learn the word of God.

The greatness of the need for people to spread the Good News about Jesus Christ was illustrated for me by an event that happened a few months before I left for the United States. A huge flood overwhelmed a large area near Calcutta, and I worked with doctors and nurses and a team from our church, going into the villages where we had schools in order to make the schools places of shelter for those whose mud houses had been completely swept away by those floods. I remember meeting one man who told me how thankful he was that the church was there for him to sleep in because he had lost his home, crops, and all his possessions. He had been living in the church for two or three weeks. I asked him whether he knew Jesus.

"No," said the man. "Who is he?"

I felt bad that I had asked the man this question at the moment of his greatest need, because it made me realize that he was missing a great source of strength in his life. I realized that there are whole areas of India, as well as other parts of the world, where people do not know about Jesus or His extraordinary message. In some villages where I've asked that question, people have suggested that I look in the next village for this person called Jesus, because he doesn't live in this one!

Nevertheless, there are some who have been reached by the message of Jesus Christ, and I have been struck by their faith. I once was part of a youth group trip to a new church known as the Fisherman's Church, located in Orissa, a state just to the south of West Bengal. The church was actually on the beach of the Bay of Bengal, and every day at nine o'clock in the morning poor fishermen with their families went into the church and worshiped God. The first church we saw was a thatched structure on the beach. When you entered this tiny shack, you couldn't see anything, because it was so dark inside compared with the bright light outside.

Even though the winters could be fairly cold, the people were virtually naked—the men wore only loincloths and the women a simple sari, while the children wore nothing. Early in the morning these fishermen would go out into the seas that were at times very rough and the pastor would pray for them. Every month, however, a few people were lost to the sea. These people had nothing but the fish they brought to the church as an offering. In spite of having so few possessions, they gave freely of what little they had, like the little boy in the United States, and it brought them enormous joy.

As Mother Teresa, who also lived and worked among the poor women and children of India, said, "The more you have, the more you are occupied, the less you give. But the less you have the more free you are. Poverty for us is a freedom. It is not a mortification, a penance. It is joyful freedom. There is no television here, no this, no that. But we are perfectly happy."

This is the message I want to convey about growing up in India and living in Calcutta. Although Calcutta has poverty and suffering of disturbing proportions, there is a reason why Dominique Lapierre's book about Calcutta is called *City of Joy*. Founded in 1690 by the Englishman Job Chamock essentially as a trading post, Calcutta, which was the capital of British India until 1910, has now grown into a thriving metropolis. Before Independence from British rule, Calcutta led India's intellectual and nationalist movements. It has often been said that one has to live in the city of Calcutta to feel its pulse. It is chaotic, volatile, noisy, and decaying. On the other hand, it is warm, indestructible, dynamic, alive, and friendly. Life in this city can be baffling for any tourist, but for a Calcuttan the spirit of this city becomes an essential part of his life. This city never ceases to intrigue all those who are inspired to visit it or spend any amount of time there.

What links the individual in Calcutta with the fisherman of Orissa is that they do not have a care in the world, mainly because they do not own anything. They do not have to worry about being robbed, because they have no money or possessions. In Calcutta and Orissa I have seen an incredible joy—and, for me, as a Christian, my burning passion has been to help poor people catch a glimpse of Jesus Christ. I believe that if they have a real encounter with the spirit of the Lord, it will make a huge difference in their lives and bring about blessing. Jesus Christ knew this when He said that the poor were blessed, that theirs would be the Kingdom of Heaven, and that in the Kingdom the first would be last and the last first (Matthew 20:16).

Both Mark Buntain and Mother Teresa helped the poor and the dying for decades in Calcutta because they believed that all of us are children of God. They knew they had both been placed by God on this earth to do good and to bring the Gospel to those who had not received it. God has chosen each of us for a mission, to know Him better and to experience His joy.

The importance of this was brought home to me by the fact that, while I had not asked to be born into a middle-class family, I knew from an early age that I was privileged. Indeed, throughout my childhood and into adolescence, I was haunted by the question of why some people had money and possessions while others had nothing. I was lucky enough to go to the Dom Bosco School, a private Roman Catholic institution and one of the most prestigious schools in Calcutta. My father was so desperate for me to get into the school that he slept in a school corridor just so that he could be one of the first to pick up an admissions form when they were handed out. While our family never wanted for anything, I was acutely aware of the enormous wealth that some students had at their disposal. I saw the wealthy driving around in their large cars and eating at expensive restaurants. This only increased my sense of the responsibility I felt to use what I had to help as many as I could, a sense of responsibility that my parents instilled in me. They expected me to be frugal and never be arrogant or boastful, for, they told me, everything I had was a blessing from God. They taught me not to take things for granted, because I might lose them the next moment.

My time with the fishermen and the poor of Calcutta taught me a very important lesson. Spending three or four days with the fishermen and their families, and sitting and eating with them, forced me to think about why they were so grateful. I hankered for material things, yet many of these people had no idea of what they were missing, if only because they had no television or radio and had never been to a city or even a large town. They had no education and an uncertain supply of food, and yet they loved God. This taught me that you do not need the pleasures or riches of the world to have the contentment and peace you can have in Jesus. You could be the poorest man on earth yet sleep like a baby through the night, simply because you have the peace of God in your life.

Mother Teresa

Growing up, I often saw the nuns from Mother Teresa's Missionaries of Charity on the street in their distinctive saris helping the poor and taking the sick to their hospices. I also saw Mother Teresa on television regularly. However, I always assumed that she was somehow inaccessible and that you needed an appointment to see her.

In my late teens I belonged to an organization called Youth for Christ. One day, I got a telephone call from the national director in Madras, who told me that one of the national directors from the United States was passing through Calcutta and needed to be shown around before he flew out the next day. "I think he wants to go and visit Mother Teresa's mission," said the director. "But just take him around in the daytime and drop him back at the airport."

Indeed, when I picked him up the next morning, the U.S. director told me he wanted to go to Mother Teresa's mission. I doubted that we would get to see her and thought that he might be satisfied by just seeing the work of the nuns. We arrived at the door and I pulled at the simple piece of string that rang the doorbell. The door was opened by a sister.

"We would like to see the work of Mother Teresa," I told her.

"Step in," she said, standing to one side to let us in. This was the first time I had set foot in Mother Teresa's home. I have been to several other homes where adults and orphans are assisted, and they are wonderful places. Yet this place had a peace that was simply transcendent. Even though there was no air conditioning or fans, there was a cool and refreshing spirit in the atmosphere.

We caught a glimpse of nuns singing and worshiping God in the chapel before we moved into a waiting room.

"Are you waiting for Mother Teresa?" someone asked us.

"Yes," I said, although I didn't quite know what to reply. Yet, after a few minutes, there standing before us was Mother Teresa. She was a tiny figure, stooped and frail. However, in spite of her size, she had an extraordinary presence. This was my first inkling of her enormous character. She had stood in a room of kings and queens, presidents and prime ministers, yet was the largest force in the room.

"Where are you from?" she asked my American friend. He told her where he was from and the kind of work he did. She put her hand on my shoulder. "There are a lot of young people who come from the United States and different parts of Europe to help there," she said. "But I don't have too many young people from India here helping me."

I didn't reply to her, but what she said stayed in my heart, and a few weeks later I started going to help out with the children in her orphanage. I had a wonderful time helping and being with the children, who were orphans waiting to be adopted. Some of my friends and I would play with them and sing songs and perform skits. When my wife and I had our own child I asked my parents to go back to the orphanage with gifts and sweets for the children, in my son's name. This is something we want to do for him on every birthday. We feel this is our way of repaying Mother Teresa's nuns for their work, and for thanking God for His blessings on us.

Mother Teresa was a huge blessing to the people and the citizens of Calcutta. Although she was born in Europe, she chose to become an Indian citizen and be buried in India. She is a testimony to what God can do through one person. When I think of Mother Teresa and her work and the work of those who follow her—every one of whom has the potential to be Mother Teresa—I am presented with an enormous challenge. All the nuns of the Missionaries of Charity left their comfortable lives and traveled to Calcutta from many parts of the world. They have decided to live a life of poverty, throwing off all honors and riches and wearing their sari and ministering to the dying. This is why I consider Mother Teresa a great leader. She implanted the same vision and dream into her followers' hearts and minds, and changed the lives of hundreds of thousands of people throughout the world.

The Missionaries of Charity's work is not confined to India, either. When I was in India, I thought the United States was a such a blessed country that there was no need of Mother Teresa's mission in America. But the Missionaries of Charity operate in the United States, and they have done enormously good work. When people ask me, "Who is the greatest person you have met?" I always answer, "Mother Teresa." I was honored to be able to spend some time with her. Mother Teresa embodied a love that was direct and expressive. As she said, "Love is a fruit in season at all times and within the reach of every hand. Anyone may gather it and no limit is set. Everyone can reach this love through meditation, prayer, sacrifice, and an intense inner life." I have always been challenged by Mother Teresa's expressions of love and faith. And as her statement illustrates, her work lives on, calling all of us to spread the message of love.

* * *

These are some of the influences on my life—my grandmother, the Assemblies of God Church, and Mother Teresa. Each of them offered me a glimpse of a life of service in the full expression of the love of God. Each of them showed me that out of enormous suffering there could not only be joy but the transformation that comes from knowing Jesus Christ. Yet it was not until I personally underwent two transformative experiences that I was to fully appreciate just how much I needed God and just what He had planned for me. One of those experiences was September 11. The other was the death of my sister.

2 ❧
Sheba's Death

W HEN PEOPLE REMEMBER my sister, Elizabeth, whom we called Sheba, they recall that she was beautiful and full of life. She was eighteen months younger than I was, and I vividly recall her joining all the games I played with the neighborhood children. She would even come out and defend me in fights! In many ways, she was a typical girl, dressing up in my mother's clothes and trying them all on. She always seemed to have a smile on her face, even though toward the end of her life she was in considerable pain from the cancer.

Elizabeth was diagnosed with leukemia in early 1983. She had not been feeling well, looked pale, and had been losing weight. We took her to our church's hospital and research center, where the medical staff conducted some tests. My father, who was working in the Middle East, came back to Calcutta and stayed with us for a few days, after which we moved Elizabeth to the Vellore Christian Medical Center (CMC), where considerable cancer research has been done, in the province of Tamil Nadu in southern India. CMC is in some ways the alma mater of medical science in India. I vividly recall going there, since it was the first time I had traveled on a plane.

The hospital had a room for us to stay in while they performed more tests. My father was also contemplating bringing Elizabeth to the States, as we wanted to try every treatment that might save her life. However, the physicians at Vellore told us that they had attempted various alternative treatments and indicated that Elizabeth was not responding well.

"She doesn't have a lot of time," they said. "We can see you are Christians. If you believe, you should start praying, for that's all that we can do."

Instead of returning to Calcutta, we went to Bangalore, where my aunt and uncle (who was a pastor) lived. We spent some time there, fasting and praying for her, before we returned to our ancestral home in Kerala, where we stayed until Elizabeth died.

While we were in Kerala, news of Sheba's illness spread far and wide, and hundreds of people visited our home to pray for her. Many of them told us that God was going to heal her, and of course that was our fervent hope. But one day, a lady pastor visited my parents. Her message was different. "Start praying for the will of God," she said. "Start praying: 'God, whatever is Your will for Elizabeth, let it happen.' "

So my father started praying for God's will to be done, and within a few weeks, my sister was dead. My father understood what was happening. The pastor was trying to prepare us for Elizabeth's departure. She wanted us to recognize that we were trying to hold on to her through our fasting and praying but that God had a plan and that His will might be different from ours. My mother found it particularly hard to accept the prayer. When she heard the new tone of my father's prayer, she told him she could not deal with anything less than Elizabeth being healed.

I remember the night Sheba died very clearly. We were in our ancestral home, a home surrounded by our relatives' houses. People had realized the end was near and had gathered around her bed. I had been taken away to the nearby home of one of my uncles, who now lives in Chicago. My family did not want me to see my sister's death. In spite of the fact that I did not have a clear idea of what was happening to her, and although I knew it was a very sad moment, I knew I had to be the room with her. So I struggled out of my uncle's grasp and ran back to my parents' house.

I saw my sister lying in her bed, surrounded by her family and the family's friends. She had known she was not well. The doctors, over the course of the previous few months, had taken many blood tests and tried chemotherapy, and had even explored the possibility of a bone transplant—a procedure that involved syringes being stuck in Elizabeth's spinal cord. We could tell that she was in great pain. Nevertheless, in those last few days, my father continuously encouraged my sister to pray. In the room, I could see a lot of people crying and offering my sister water. "Sheba, say Praise the Lord, say Jesus," my father was saying. "Say Thank you Jesus." As she began to slip away, my father asked her to repeat these words over and over. My father led his daughter into death, and to this day I do not know where he found the strength to do it. My father believes his strength came from God. The final word on her lips was "Jesus," after which she closed her eyes.

At that moment, I realized that she was going to die. I pushed my way to her bedside and cried out at the top of my voice:

"Sheba!" To my amazement, she opened her eyes and looked at me and the other people in the room. Then she closed her eyes and never opened them again. To my childish mind, it was as if her soul had departed through a window or door somewhere and could be caught and brought back. This was the way I tried to understand what was incomprehensible to me: the death of my beloved sister.

Why?

We never truly discussed Sheba's death and its effect on the family. My father tried to remain as strong as he was on the day Elizabeth died, to hold himself together for the sake of the family. He would project a very mature image just for my mother and me and for other members of our family, but we all could tell that he was struggling deeply with his sadness and endeavoring not to show it to people. However, a few days after Sheba's death, he started breaking down and crying. No one wanted to see the pictures taken at the funeral, yet I know my father sometimes looked at her dolls and toys and the clothes she used to wear.

On some deep level, we knew that Elizabeth was with God, and this was something we *did* talk about. When she was buried, the pastor commented on how much peace there was at the funeral, because we were not mourning like people who had no hope. "We mourn because we have lost our loved one," he said. "But we rejoice because we are going to see her in heaven." That statement has always stuck with me, not only because it was something I heard in the funeral service and my father always talked about it, but because it has provided me with great comfort ever since. After a few months, and with great difficulty and reluctance, my father returned to his work in the Middle East.

My mother reacted to Elizabeth's death by falling sick, and there was a time when we were afraid we might lose her as well.

Although my mother was hospitalized and her condition was diagnosed as a thyroid disorder, it is clear to me that the sickness was at least partly psychosomatic. She stopped eating, took to her bed, and experienced all kinds of opportunistic infections. She had the same confidence as my father that Sheba was with God, but in many ways she had been forced to travel a longer journey than my father toward acceptance. He had been more easily able to reconcile Elizabeth's approaching death with the recognition that whatever happened would be the will of God. Eventually, my mother recovered. But none of us was ever the same again.

In spite of the enormous suffering they were experiencing, my parents never showed any bitterness toward God. This was something that I could not reconcile myself with. My parents loved God, gave to God, and were involved in building His Kingdom on earth. And yet their daughter was taken away. Why her? I asked. Why did it have to be *my* sister who was taken away? Why couldn't it have been someone else—someone who hurt or killed other people? Why did people who did those things enjoy life while my sister had died?

I was angry at the fact that death could snatch anybody away and there was no way they could be brought back—that no amount of money or earthly power could alter that fact. I felt my life was over, that there would never be any kind of fun in the house again, that there would always be the shadow of my sister's death in our family. Positive thoughts and good things seemed impossibly far off to me.

I bottled all these feelings up inside me and shunned every effort, even from my grandmother, to talk with me about them. From the time of my sister's death, when I was eight, until I was in my early teens, I did not talk about what had happened. I ran away from every conversation about it, partly because I didn't want to see my parents become upset and partly because it stirred up too much sadness inside me. Many of the friends I went to school with had no idea what I was feeling, or that I had even lost a sister. I kept to myself and stayed away from girls, because I didn't want to get too close to anyone who might remind me of her.

Throughout this time, we continued to go to church and I went to Sunday School. But I was only going through the motions. God for me was a bully—a being who could take away people on a whim. And I felt I could not argue with Him because I was scared He would do the same thing to me that He had done to Sheba. I felt powerless. Even after my transforming experience with Mark Buntain, to which I will come shortly, I probably acted out of that sense of frustration. I was a difficult adolescent. I didn't want anyone to interfere in my life; I reacted very badly against anyone telling me what to do (especially my mother, who was fiercely protective of me and restricted what I could do with my friends, probably because she did not want to lose me). I never completely went off the rails because of my fear of God. But I was unfocused at school, and the early teens is a period when a lot of kids get into things they shouldn't. Because of my behavior and the period of my life I was going through, my father felt he should be there to parent me along with my mother. My father gave up his job in the Middle East and came home to be with his family.

In the decades since Elizabeth's death, as I have grown older I have come, through God's help, to understand the loss I felt. When your loved ones die, you are left with an enormous void in your heart. The only thing you have are your memories of the one who died, and the hurt of your loss can take forever to heal. Our life throws up innumerable kinds of disappointments and discouragements, as well as presenting us with positive experiences and periods of joy. Over time, these disappointments and discouragements can be forgotten and the joys can fade. But you never forget the loss of a loved one, especially someone as close to you as Sheba was to my parents and me. From that time on I could feel, along with my own misery, the unfathomable depth of my parents' suffering and the pain they felt at losing their only daughter.

A Decision for Christ

After my sister's death, I felt alienated from God, unable to forgive Him for what I felt was His unfair removal of Sheba from my life. But there were two incidents that began to signal a turn for me in my relationship with Christ. Both incidents involved in some way my opening my heart to Him, or making a decision for Christ.

I first made a decision for Christ when I was twelve or thirteen years old. I was in church and saw one of my best friends making a decision for God. The pastor called out, "Whoever wants Jesus, especially young people, this is your time. Just raise your hand, and we will pray for you and encourage you." My friend raised his hand, and I could see that the church was excited that this young man had made that commitment. Then another boy of the same age did the same. I looked around and saw that I was the only boy in the group who hadn't raised his hand. I felt an enormous internal pressure to do it, if only because these two contemporaries of mine seemed to feel something, and I thought that if they could give their hearts, then perhaps I should as well. I didn't want people around me to think that I was the only one who didn't want to make a decision for Christ. So up went my hand.

Those who had made a commitment were told to stand up, and the pastor led us into a prayer for forgiveness. People around me were praying and I felt very connected to the assembly. I can't say that I kept my promise to live a sin-free life after that, and looking back, I can see that I was pressured by the situation into putting my hand up and that I did not enter into it with a full heart. Nevertheless, I believe this first occasion primed me for a much more important and significant commitment I was to make a few years later—one that was given without reservation and without a sense of punishment if I refused.

I was about fourteen or fifteen years old and attending a Vacation Bible School (VBS) class, which we were privileged to have taught by Mark Buntain himself. At that stage of his life, Mark Buntain was in his sixties, a big man with large hands and a booming voice. He had very expressive gestures, which he used to great effect in his preaching. I rode the elevator with him occasionally, and although awestruck I felt very close to him. He seemed to be constantly engaged in conversation, intense prayer, and worship with God, speaking in tongues and in communication with God all the time. That particular day, Mark Buntain was commenting on the textual passage where Jesus performs the miracle of feeding the five thousand people who had come to hear him speak with only five loaves and two fishes (John 6:1–14).

Mark Buntain's message was simple. "Jesus," he said, "could have used the adults assembled to find the food. There would have been people who had the means to buy food, but none of them had the answer or the solution. Instead, a simple child," whom Mark Buntain called Johnnie so that we could relate to him, "had a solution to feed five thousand people. There was a great lesson in that," he continued. "When God wants miracles to happen, He doesn't care about your age or background or the way you are. What matters is your heart. Johnnie," he said, "had nothing but this small amount of food. But it was he whom Jesus chose to use in order to perform the miracle of the multiplication.

"There are people who are hurt here," he said. And I felt as though Mark Buntain was talking directly to me. "There are young people for whom God has a destiny. But for God to use you in that dimension, whatever you have you need to give."

For years, I had thought of myself as having few talents. I was neither the most intelligent person nor the most popular, neither the best at public speaking nor the most sociable. I didn't have any obvious gifts, such as being able to play a musical instrument or being a great athlete. Yet here I was being told that it didn't matter, that God was calling me to the altar not in spite of the hurt and resentment I felt at Him and my old, entrenched habits, but *because* of them.

For years, many godly men and women had told me that there was a special purpose for and call on my life. "Young man," they would say, "you've been separated from your mother's womb for something." They would tell me that when my mother was pregnant with me, she had fallen ill with chicken pox and feared that I would die or be born with a disability. They indicated to me that God had a plan for me because I had survived the birth intact. "God is going to take you to places and you will travel the world," they would say. But I did not know what was in store for me, although I sensed that there would be a turning point. However, I had no idea when it would be and was impatient for it to happen.

As Mark Buntain told the story of the child called by Jesus to help perform miracles (John 6:9), I felt an enormous tug on my heart. Everything around me disappeared, and it felt as though that sermon—out of the hundreds of sermons I had heard in my life—was directed only at me. It was as if Mark Buntain was speaking straight to my heart, and every word he said applied completely to my life, my past, and my future, what I wanted to do and where I wanted to go. All around me there were people responding to his message, but I felt that the message was solely for me. I experienced a great need to be the first person at the altar and almost ran to the front of the church.

At the altar, there were children of all ages. I remember that after Mark Buntain finished the prayer of forgiveness, he started praying for people. He laid his right hand on my head and lifted his left hand in the air. "Young man," he said to me, "God is going to change the destiny of your life. He is going to use you for millions of people."

Immediately I felt God working in my heart. Something warm began burning within me and I could feel all my old anxieties and resentments emptying out of me and relief flooding through me. I was overwhelmed by a sense of joy and a powerful anointing coming upon my life. I felt a connection with God. I had, as I said, tried to be a good Christian. Yet I knew I had also been going through the motions, showing people the mask of faith. Now the mask had fallen, and here I was before God, telling Him how much I needed His help.

The anxieties I had about my lack of talents melted away, and in their place came a sense of destiny, of purpose. I realized that I had a mission, which would one day reveal itself in its fullness. And I knew—even at that moment at the altar—that God was birthing in me a burden, a responsibility for lost people. Mark Buntain told us that God's message was "Give what you have for God and God will use that and touch millions of people."

I prayed to God, "If You can use that young boy in the feeding of the five thousand people, use me. I have no idea how You are going to use me, but just as I am, use me." And it was at that moment that I understood all the predictions that had been made about my destiny. I still only had a vague understanding of what that destiny was, but I felt that God was preparing me for it. Even as days turned into weeks and weeks into months and years after the day when I gave my heart to the Lord, I knew there would be a turning point when things were going to change. I had no idea that they would take the shape they did.

A Greater Sense of Mission

From that time on, my life changed. I became more sociable and more popular among my peers. While I did slip back at times into a life of aimless consumption, I nevertheless became more aware of those less fortunate than myself, especially through my work in the youth group. I became heavily involved in the church and started learning the word of God, through daily reading of the Bible and memorizing scripture.

I began to notice that, in spite of my earlier belief, I had hidden talents. I was voted onto the Youth Council of our church, which was considered very prestigious, because everybody had to vote for you. I was utterly amazed: here were all these people voting for me, even though I had only been involved in the Youth Council for a comparatively short time. I was on the Youth Council for a year before I became the Youth President for the church. As President I was responsible for leading, along with our youth pastor, a group of young people on field trips and in various activities. It was on one of these field trips that we visited the fisherfolk of Orissa whom I described in Chapter One.

On Sunday afternoons, a group of friends and I started going into the hospitals in Calcutta with religious pamphlets and to visit sick people. One afternoon I was in a state government hospital with a friend of mine who had a guitar with him, because we had just come from church, where he used to play. There was a group of 150 to 200 children gathered around the hospital because their parents lived and worked there. Something in my heart told me to go and talk to the children. I gathered my friends together and we went over to where the kids were playing and began singing. Soon there were twice as many children around us, listening to our songs and watching the little plays that we put on. We sang Bible songs and performed small skits on parables. Because they were children of Hindu and Muslim backgrounds, we made sure our songs and skits stayed on broad themes of good versus evil and not on any religion in particular.

The children were so enchanted that they refused to let us go. Finally, I told the children that we would be back at the same time the following week. My friends and I began a little weekend program entertaining and teaching the children while their families worked. When I moved away from Calcutta, we handed the program over to the church.

Being with these children deepened my gratitude to God and enhanced my sense of the profound relationship that God has with children. Through being with the children, I was able to connect with and see the needs of those who would come and talk to us about their suffering and what they were going through. Many of them had fathers who drank, who beat them and their mothers. They had no food to eat or proper schools to go to. They were five to nine years old, and some of the older children would bring their baby brothers and sisters with them and carry them on their laps. Once in a while we would bring the children candy and toys, which we bought with our pocket money. Over time, the parents would come and see what we were doing, and soon we had a very good relationship with that community. The whole experience taught me something that has stuck with me for the rest of my life: God uses children in many places to be an instrument for His blessings to be poured upon a family. He makes them instruments of His saving grace, as I discovered in Mark Buntain's homily on the feeding of the five thousand. It was heartbreaking and yet inspiring at the same time. Once more, amid the suffering and deprivation there was joy and a deep sense of God's work in the world.

That is why our missionary schools have been such a blessing in many parts of the world, including North America and Europe. The schools we have set up have been tools for transformation. The lives of parents, children, communities, and whole nations have changed because of the education our schools and others like them have provided. Ever since I met those children, God has placed in my heart the realization that, as Jesus understood, children are the keys to the Kingdom of God, and if you can touch them at a young age with the Gospel of Jesus, you have touched them forever.

I left Calcutta after I finished my bachelor's degree in commerce at St. Xavier's College and enrolled in the Masters of Business Administration (MBA) course at the Indian Institute of Planning and Management in New Delhi. New Delhi, the capital of India, was a very different experience for me, since it was the first time I had lived away from my parents. Although there were moments when I went away from God when I was in New Delhi, it was also a time of learning and refreshment. It was there that I came to the important realization that when you don't have God's peace in your life, you don't have anything.

After I graduated, I started work in marketing at a company specializing in trade promotion and organization. But I began to feel lonely in Delhi and felt I needed to be back where my family was. After a few months I got a marketing job with a tire company in Calcutta.

It was at this point that two enormous opportunities opened up for me, opportunities that would change my life and begin the path on which I have now started. The first of these began with a telephone conversation. On the other end of the telephone line was a young woman who, though I didn't know it at the time, was to become my wife.

3
Coming to America

I MET MY wife Mary in an unusual way. My father and her father had grown up together as neighbors in the same town in Kerala. Although I had never met Mary, I knew her father to be a man of integrity. In some ways, it could be said that we had an arranged marriage, because, although Mary and I were completely opposed to arranged marriages, we did not have a conventional courtship. Arranged marriages are still relatively common in India, and there are both pros and cons to them. A lot of arranged marriages have been successful. Indeed, my parents had an arranged marriage and it has worked wonderfully well.

Nevertheless, when the proposal was made by someone who suggested that Mary and I would make a good couple, I told my father that there was no way I was going to marry someone in an arranged marriage, and Mary said the same thing to her father. Because Mary lived with her family in New Jersey, having emigrated to the United States when she was six, and I lived in Calcutta, we both felt it was important that we meet up and see whether we liked each other before we took such a major step.

My father showed me her picture. "Dad," I said. "In her picture she looks beautiful. But I want to know her a little better and have a brief courtship and then see where we are going." Mary said the same to her father.

One day, Mary's father called me up. "Here's Mary," he said, "she wants to talk to you." And we began to talk. I asked her for her email address, and from that time on we started writing to each other every day. You could say that we fell in love over email, because our emails became more and more frequent and we began talking on the phone every other day. My job required me to travel out of Calcutta a lot, but I used to make sure that I came back each night in time to write an email to Mary before she started work the next day.

In this way Mary and I became very attached to each other. The plan had been that Mary would come from New Jersey to Calcutta for a friend's wedding, and that we would meet then and have a proper courtship. However, as it turned out, before Mary even arrived in India we had fallen in love over the phone and the Internet, and what would have been a courtship in India turned into preparations for our marriage. It was something I couldn't fathom! I didn't understand how I could have fallen in love with someone I had not even met face to face! We did spend some time together in Kerala before we were married and, indeed, as soon as we met, all my feelings for her were confirmed. I found everything I was looking for in her, and I hope she could say the same thing about me!

Throughout my courtship and the time leading up to my marriage, prayer was essential for me. The words of Paul—"Let the peace of Christ rule in your hearts" (Colossians 3:15)—have been a guiding light in any decision I make regarding my career, my marriage, my family life, and my future. If I feel God's peace about some decision, I believe that God is trying to tell me what I should be doing. In this case, I felt the peace of God ruling out all of the doubts and questions I had.

Mary and I were married on January 27, 2001, at the Mark Buntain Memorial Assemblies of God Church in Calcutta. Coming to India was eye-opening for her. Although she had been born in India, she had lived in the United States with her family since she was six years old. She had visited a few times since then, but never for such an extended length of time.

Mary and I shared a commitment to God, something that was very important for me. I had always known that the person I married would have to share this same commitment, because if we were pulling in different directions our marriage was not going to be harmonious. God was always first for me in my life, and I expected Him to be first for Mary. Mary was second in importance for me, as I was for her.

Mary and I understood that our marriage opened up an enormous opportunity for us; we would both be able to live and work in the United States, where Mary was a citizen. Mary had just finished college in accounting and was between jobs. So we were, in some ways, both starting somewhere new.

Before I married Mary, I had never thought much about moving to the United States. But the image of immigrants—especially from India—coming to the United States and succeeding was one that attracted me, perhaps because it was familiar. That said, it was still a difficult decision, mainly because I had a strong community in Calcutta. I was involved with my church, I had friends and a good job, and, since the death of my sister, I was my parents' only child. Indeed, my parents were initially not very eager for me to move to the United States, because they feared they would be lonely. However, they understood that my prospects might be improved by spending some time working in the U.S.

It took a year for the visa process to be completed. During that time, I read a lot about life in the U.S. and the American media, which I was familiar with through watching CNN and other American news channels. I felt I already knew a great deal about the United States, not merely because of my exposure to it through the media, but because a lot of people from the United States who passed through Calcutta visited our church and expressed their support for us. But, like many people around the world, I was struck by the image of America that I saw on television.

I have always been concerned with current affairs and in learning what is going on all over the world. As the events of September 11 showed all of us, what happens in supposedly remote corners of the world can have an impact anywhere in the world in some way. I was also interested in the United States because, like India, it is a democracy. By sheer force of numbers enfranchised, India is the world's largest democracy, while the United States is the most powerful.

What struck me in watching American television was the dedication to the protection of individual lives. I was amazed that television programs would feature efforts by federal or state agencies to rescue individuals trapped by circumstances—whether in a flood or a fire, in a snowdrift or an accident. An enormous amount of resources, time, and manpower would be expended in rescuing that one person. For me, as an Indian, that was significant, because when there were catastrophic accidents or natural disasters in India, the government, mainly because it lacked resources, would be unable to do much to help the situation. Furthermore, if the government did try to do something there would be problems with coordination and corruption. I often used to feel that in India unless fifty or a hundred people died in a tragedy, it was somehow deemed not worthy of coverage by the media.

There were aspects of American culture that were confusingly contradictory. The impression we received in India from the news programs that beamed out of the U.S. was of a country that was confident of its power throughout almost the entire world. It was a prosperous nation, yet one that placed a great deal of value on human life. However, there were other types of media that did not present a positive image, such as MTV. MTV presented a highly sexualized and commercialized worldview that emphasized having things over the dignity and wishes of individual people. MTV encouraged many young Indians with money in the 1980s and 1990s simply to enjoy themselves and not commit themselves to any larger goals than making money and having fun.

The influence of American popular culture is pervasive in India, as it is throughout the world. If you were to walk onto the campus of a university in India, you would find it not much different from a campus in the United States. There are the same clothes, the same language, and often the same attitudes. Of course, this transfer of culture is not a one-way street; such Indian cultural expressions as yoga and meditation and Ayurvedic medicine have made extensive inroads in American culture. Clearly our worlds are coming together in important and challenging ways that will, I hope, increase our mutual understanding. Nevertheless, I believe strongly that no culture should dominate another and that we need to respect each other's cultural traditions. Even though the influence of MTV was not positive, other U.S. television outlets, such as the Discovery and Learning channels, opened up for me a real sense of how culturally rich and diverse the U.S. is, and how broad is its scientific and industrial knowledge-base.

So I knew the United States as a land of immigrants—a land where people who had fled oppression or economic disadvantage had been absorbed and had prospered. I knew that a great many Indians had come to America and been very successful, and I knew North Americans as a generous and compassionate people. It had been shown to me through the work of people like Mark and Huldah Buntain, who brought their energy and commitment to preaching and healing when they could have lived a comfortable life at home. It had been shown to me through the amount of money pledged by congregations throughout the United States to our church, and churches like us, working in India and throughout the developing world to alleviate the suffering of the poor and sick and to spread the Gospel of Jesus Christ. As I discovered when I arrived, and especially on September 11, that belief in the generosity of the American people was fully justified.

America

I touched down in the United States on February 26, 2001, during one of the coldest spells of what seemed to be a particularly cold winter. I recall that there was a snowstorm that day, and my wife had brought a jacket for me to wear. I had never experienced this kind of cold before, and she was worried I might fall sick.

After a weeklong break, Mary, who had just landed a job at a large financial services company, had to go back to work, and I was stuck at home. Even though I was eager to get out of the house and see this new country, I was unable to do so, because it snowed for the next two or three days. I had little money and some trepidation, but a lot of hope. (I didn't have much money because the conversion rates between Indian rupees and U.S. dollars were such that it didn't make sense to convert the one to the other.) It was quite a shock to arrive in a country in such circumstances, especially when I had had a good job, a good income, and a good lifestyle in my home country. Mary and I lived with her parents while we saved enough money to find an apartment of our own. I wanted to live with my wife in our own home, and to get a car, and felt that I had to start earning money as soon as I could. For that, of course, I needed a job. Consequently, I began accompanying Mary in the mornings when she went to work in Manhattan.

Mary's job was in the World Trade Center, and every day I would use the Twin Towers as a starting point for going out and walking around New York City to get a feel for the place. I had no idea of the layout of Manhattan or how the subway worked. I just walked. However, I decided always to keep within a safe distance of the Twin Towers so I wouldn't get lost.

This was my first indication of how significant the Twin Towers of the World Trade Center were to the people of New York City. You would never be lost if you could locate the World Trade Center, because the towers were so tall that they often stood above any buildings around you. Every lunchtime I would return to the World Trade Center and have lunch with my wife in a special spot we had designated. There was a little marble monument, a gift from a European city to New York, that was on the mezzanine level of the south tower where we always met. Even after I got a job in the World Trade Center, we would make that our spot.

Although I had a Green Card, I did not have a social security number until two weeks after I first landed in the United States. Now I was ready to find work. Everyone—my wife, our relatives, and others whom I met—kept telling me that it was going to take a long time and that it wasn't easy to get a job in New York, especially in the recession that was going on at the time. I was a very recent immigrant, they argued, and everything was new for me. I should spend more time settling in and getting to understand the culture and the usual ways of doing things before I rushed out and tried to find a job. I didn't have any U.S. work experience, they pointed out. I should take it easy and keep out of the cold, because walking around the city in the middle of winter was a sure way of getting sick.

I was desperate to start work as soon as possible and refused to believe that I couldn't find a job quickly. This was New York, I thought! There are always jobs if you are in the right place at the right time and you look hard enough. From the second week onward, I printed out copies of my resume and walked around Manhattan looking for recruitment agencies that could help me find work. Many temp agencies took my resume and told me they would keep me on file. But I wanted to work in marketing and had no interest in a temporary job. I became discouraged at the fact that I couldn't find an agency that catered to people who wanted to work in my field of interest.

I was also discouraged by just how cold it was. As I walked all over Manhattan, I felt at times as though I was going to freeze to death. I remember one day especially. It was pouring freezing rain and I felt my hands going numb. I had no idea what to do. I'm going to die in this cold, I thought. I decided to stay for an hour or so in indoor public spaces, just to warm myself up, before setting out to begin looking for a job. One of those places was the New York Stock Exchange, where I saw the people trading and conducting business. I felt as though I was at the nerve center of something very powerful and full of energy, like the core of a nuclear reactor. Millions of transactions were being made in an instant. This, I thought to myself, is where the world comes to do business. I was struck by the vast amount of wealth in the United States, especially as represented by lower Manhattan. Sometimes it moved me to tears, because I thought of the life back in India, and how incredibly privileged Americans were to have such riches.

In spite of all my efforts on the streets and in using the Internet, I was getting nowhere and getting more and more depressed. I couldn't believe that I was unable to get a job in my area of interest. It was at this point that the World Trade Center once more entered my life.

Getting a Job

It was in March 2001, about a month after arriving in New York, that during one of my trips to the World Trade Center with Mary I saw that there was a job fair being conducted at the Marriott Hotel at the World Trade Center. I had never been to a job fair before. Because I had been looking for a job every day, I was wearing a suit and had my resume with me. I simply walked into the fair and began looking around.

Everywhere were financial and life insurance companies who seemed to be interested in hiring me and wanting me to join them as a salesman working on commission, since my skills seemed to match their requirements. However, I really wanted to work in marketing and so ended up approaching the representatives of two telecommunications companies who told me that they would be interested in interviewing me.

The representative from one of the companies, Heidi Inzerillo, took my resume and told me that her office was on the eighty-first floor of the north tower of the World Trade Center. Although she told me that the fair was neither the time nor the place to conduct an interview, she said that if I gave her a call she could set up a time and date. "Let's do it now," I said eagerly. "Let's get a date." So we set a date, and she told how to get to her floor. "Security is tight," she said, "so you need to have an ID," something I didn't have at the time. As it turned out, I used my credit card, because it had my photograph on it.

I was very excited at the prospect of being able to work at the World Trade Center, because my wife worked there. I also knew it as a symbol of New York and of the United States. At that point, I didn't know much about the company or the position for which I was applying. But the fact that I was interviewing at the World Trade Center on the eighty-first floor meant a lot.

When I arrived at the office of the telecommunications company, Heidi ushered me into the conference room and asked me to wait until the branch manager was ready to interview me. As I sat there, Heidi asked me whether I had seen the Statue of Liberty. When I said I hadn't, she was delighted.

"Well," she said. "We have an awesome view of the Statue of Liberty. Do you want to take a look?"

Heidi took me to a corner of the conference room. It was a bright, sunny spring morning. Through the glass windows of the Towers I saw the pleasure cruisers passing Liberty Island. I thought it was the most beautiful sight I had ever seen. I had previously only seen the Statue of Liberty on television, or in posters and magazines. And here I was, actually looking at it with my own eyes! I had been considering taking a ferry to Liberty Island to see the statue, and I had read about its history and seen boat trips going out to the island from Battery Park. I had even told myself that Mary and I should take a trip to see it together, as a way of introducing me to America. To me and to millions of immigrants from all over the world, the statue was a symbol of America. It meant freedom and possibility and the gateway to the vast potential of life in America. The history of America and the Statue of Liberty went together, and I was seeing it from, of all places, the World Trade Center.

My interview went well, and I was invited back for a second one. The day before my second interview I went to church and prayed to God. "God," I said, "I need to start my life here. And I have heard how in order to get a job you need to know the right people in the right places, and I don't know anyone." And I asked God to hear my prayer for a job. I believe that God heard my prayer, for the next day I was told I had satisfied the interviewers and had got the job. I would be working for a telecommunications company on the eighty-first floor of the north tower of the World Trade Center.

When I wrote and called my friends and family in India to tell them how I had landed a job so quickly, in the World Trade Center, in the same complex where my wife worked, everyone was amazed. On later reflection, I find it significant that I didn't need to explain where I worked, because everybody in Calcutta knew what the World Trade Center was and could imagine it in their mind's eye. I told them I could see the Statue of Liberty from the office, and that for my friends was a sign that I had made it, that I had become successful in the United States. But all the time, I knew that it was God's grace that had allowed me to get the job and that it was He who had done this for me.

On April 14, 2001, I began my job at the telecommunications company. I loved working at the World Trade Center, because Mary and I would travel to work together in the morning, eat our lunch at our favorite location on the mezzanine level of the south tower, and meet up at different times of the day in the building complex. Just after I began work there, I saw maintenance people changing the flowers as a sign of spring beginning.

Soon the whole building was decorated with bright, colorful flowers, something that filled me with joy and made me appreciate just how well maintained the building was. It never ceased to amaze me just how much you could do within the confines of the World Trade Center. There was a post office where we could mail our letters and get stamps. There were banks and restaurants. There was a huge shopping mall on the lower level of the World Trade Center that was so large that it spread beneath the entire complex. There was a subway station—on the E line—that stopped underneath the World Trade Center, and the place even had its own zip code.

Every day I would ride the bus from my home in New Jersey to Port Authority. Then I would take the E train directly to my place of work. An elevator would carry me to the seventy-eighth floor, where the sky deck that overlooked Manhattan was, and another elevator took me an additional three floors to my office. Each morning when I entered the building I would see the ticket booth on the ground level and all the tourists lining up to visit the observatory. It made me feel proud that my wife and I actually worked at the place where hundreds of thousands of people each year would come to visit and take pictures of the city or the towers with their video recorders and cameras. When Mary and I went outside into the courtyard of the World Trade Center—which would be full of people meeting and eating lunch or listening to the concerts that often took place in the afternoons and evenings—we frequently saw tourists lying flat on the ground taking pictures of their family or friends with the Twin Towers behind them. I remember telling Mary that we should have some pictures taken of us in our work clothes to send our friends and family. As it turns out, we never got around to doing it before it was too late.

A couple of weeks into my new job I had to travel to Boston for a training session. When I was in the airport, flying out of La Guardia, it struck me just how many flights there were to different parts of the United States. I made a commitment at that point to visit as much of the United States as I could, figuring that it would only be business commitments that could take me to certain places, since it would be expensive to travel as a tourist. I calculated that it would probably take me twenty or twenty-five years to see the states. Little did I know that in less than a year I would end up seeing most of the country.

Insurance for Life

On Friday, September 7, 2001, I met for lunch a woman named Siu Ming Lau, who had introduced herself earlier to me as a life insurance agent. I told her a little bit about my background, that I was married and that Mary was pregnant, and Siu asked me whether I had any life insurance. I replied that I felt covered by my office, but she added that, while the coverage was adequate, I should probably have some further coverage of my own.

Although I didn't have much of a sense of the financial markets in the United States, Siu patiently talked about how important it was that my family be covered. I didn't need much convincing. I was going to have a child and, although I was reluctant to sign anything that required me to hand over money, something in my heart told me to get it done. So, on that Friday, I met Siu for lunch and decided to fill out the paperwork. I vividly recall Siu telling me, after I had completed the form, "Touch wood, you get out of this place, you're insured for life."

Writing the check for my life insurance was the hardest check I had ever had to write. That night I told Mary about the policy. She was not pleased. "I really don't think you should do this life insurance policy," she said. First, she said, we were so young, and second, why was I thinking of death? I told her that I would bring the papers home so that she could read them and see what she would have to do to activate the policy in case of an emergency. I would pick up the papers for her when I got back to work on Monday.

On Monday, September 10, I was scheduled to take my driving test. The previous Friday, my office workers had been teasing me about the test—which I feared I might fail since in India I was used to driving on the left-hand side of the road!—and demanding that if I passed I would show them my mug shot for my license. That night, after I had passed, Mary and I went over to her parents' house to celebrate. the fact I had passed my test. Curiously, Mary and I stayed longer than we usually did. We kept on thinking that once we were back at our apartment, we would have to go to sleep and then get up the next morning and go back to work. We had had such a nice long weekend (Mary had taken the day off work so we could be together) that we didn't want it to end. So, reluctantly and wearily, we arrived at our apartment and climbed into bed just after midnight on the morning of September 11, 2001.

4 🌿
September 11, 2001

THE MORNING OF September 11 was beautifully sunny. Mary, who was fourteen weeks pregnant, had been having a hard time in recent days. She felt nauseated, found sleeping difficult, and became tired walking only a few blocks. In the previous few weeks, instead of going with me to work every day, Mary had been sleeping longer, getting up later, and coming to work on her own. I missed sharing our early morning commute, because it gave us a chance to talk. Our jobs were very busy and stressful, and I found the pace strange and difficult, since business in India was conducted at a much less intense and frantic speed. My wife and I were often too tired in the evening to spend much time together or talk much before we had to go to sleep. The mornings had provided that opportunity.

That morning, however, Mary got up at the same time as I did. She wanted to go in early to talk with her supervisor and find out who had taken care of her work on her day off. Nevertheless, we did not go to work together, since I had to be at work earlier than she did. I left the house about forty-five minutes ahead of Mary. As usual, I took the bus and dozed a little, waking up (also as usual) just as the World Trade Center came into view across the Hudson River.

I was the second person to arrive at my office on the eighty-first floor that morning. My manager was the only one there at 7:30. Slowly people started trickling in, asking me whether I had passed my driving test and then demanding jokingly to see my photo on my newly issued driving license. Soon I found my license passing through the entire office, with everyone wanting to see the picture, and then everybody in turn taking out their licenses and showing their own. When I look back, I am struck by how much life and good humor there was in this ordinary inter-action between people in an office as they began their day. At about eight o'clock, as part of our regular morning ritual, I called Mary on my cell phone and found out that she was dozing on the bus and had just come into view of the Towers. "I'll call you when I get to the Towers," she said.

I vividly remember that at four minutes past eight o'clock that morning, on a day full of ironies, I sent an email to a friend of mine, Thomas Sirinides. This is what I wrote.

Hi Tom,
Great to hear that you are feeling great in the Lord now. It's so strange...you were feeling the same way that I was on Sunday. I had some problems myself and could not release myself during worship, and it was only after service that I felt God doing a work in me.

September 11, 2001

Tom, this is my sixth month here in this country. God has been so good to us in so many ways. He's been so good. But there is a major issue that I am trying to deal with.

Back in India, although I had a job in the secular field, I was so involved in ministry. If the church doors were open I would be there. I was working with the young people in our church there and now here all I find myself doing is going to church on Sunday. I am so ashamed to admit that I am not involved in any avenue of ministry. Maybe this is what God wants me to go through right now. Waiting for His will and purpose.

So please keep us in your prayers. I know I have a call of God on my life and this is not a good phase of life that I am going through.

Would appreciate your prayers.
May God bless and all that you touch be blessed today.
In His Grace,
Sujo

I then received a call from a colleague in our office in Philadelphia who had been in training with me. He wanted me to fax him some papers. I made photocopies of the documents I was going to fax, went over to the fax machine, and began to fax them through. It was 8:45 a.m.

Attack

American Airlines Flight 11 bound from Boston to Los Angeles, with a full tank of fuel and carrying sixty-four people, crashed into the north tower, or Tower One, of the World Trade Center at 8:46 a.m. The Boeing 767 plane struck with full force between the ninety-fourth and ninety-eighth floors of the 110-floor building. However, because of the size of the plane and its tilt, the five or six floors on either side of the plane were directly affected by the impact.

There was a colossal explosion. The windows immediately shattered, causing papers and debris to fly out and be blown into our office. As the plane struck, we could feel the building tilting to the left at the force of the impact, and the steel girders that supported all the floors creaked. I could see fireballs shooting out of the building, and the ceiling above me and the walls around me started cracking and bowing. Fires began to break out all over our floor.

Although we were in shock, we rapidly realized what had happened, even though we did not know why. We knew that it unlikely that a bomb had caused such an impact at such an altitude. One of my colleagues yelled out, "It's a plane!" just as the plane struck. Many of us had heard the sound of an airplane's engines becoming increasingly louder, and just before the point of contact the sound had been deafening—so something seemed amiss. None of us had expected this, however. The World Trade Center had been the site of a previous attack in 1993, when terrorists placed a truck bomb in the basement of the complex, and six people had died. Thus, people were extra aware of security measures. However, most of my office had begun work in the World Trade Center after 1993, so they were less aware of the possibility of a terrorist attack. Nevertheless, the thought of terrorists flashed through our minds.

But we had more immediate fears. As soon as the plane hit I had been thrown to the floor with my face flat on the carpet. My immediate thought was that the building was going to collapse and that I was going to die. I'm never going to see my wife or my parents again, I said to myself. I'm never going to see the face of my unborn child. I started praying that God would do something miraculous to save us. All around me people were shrieking and crying. Because of the size and angle of the plane, different parts of the building had been affected differently. The area where my desk was, and where I had been sitting just a few moments before, had been destroyed, while the area by the fax machine was relatively intact, even though there was smoke and fire everywhere.

Our telecommunications company shared its office space with a financial services company. Workers at that company were the first to find the exit to the stairwell, and they broke the door down to get in. Initially, they had tried to douse the flames with fire extinguishers, but they rapidly came to the conclusion that such attempts were useless.

We all gathered together and made our way to the stairwell. The World Trade Center was designed with the elevators in the middle of the building, with offices surrounding them. As we stepped out of our office, we could see flames, stoked by the jet fuel that was pouring down the shafts, shooting out of the elevators; the doors had buckled and given way. Keeping ourselves as near to the edge of the wall as we could, we passed the elevators and reached the stairwell.

We began to run and walk as quickly as we could down the stairwell, which was so narrow that we could only move in pairs side by side. I immediately noticed that there were relatively few people coming behind us from the floors above, and my heart sank as I tried to imagine the devastation above me. As more and more people from the floors below us joined us on the stairwell, our pace slowed. It was difficult to know which floor we were on, even though we initially made very quick progress down the stairwell. There were conflicting theories about what had happened just minutes earlier. But there was one thought that was never countenanced once we left our offices and moved closer to the ground: that the building we were in would collapse.

As I made my way down the stairwell, I looked at my watch, and my heart became even heavier. I realized that Mary usually got to work at 8:45, and that, on this day of all days, she had set off for work a little earlier than usual. I had no idea what had happened to the other building, or whether the plane that had hit our building had also hit hers. But I feared the very worst.

I tried to call Mary on my cell phone but was unable to connect with her. I began to feel desperate, even though my colleagues tried to reassure me and to determine whether I was sure that Mary was in the other tower. All around me people were helping each other down the stairwell, comforting those who were beginning to panic, and expressing their gratitude at being able to get out. Every now and again, we would step aside and lean against the wall to allow the injured, burned, or elderly to go ahead of us down the stairwell. In our thoughts were those passengers on the plane, who we knew could not be alive.

The Fifty-third Floor

In spite of the comforting words of my friends, I knew that they knew no more of what had happened than I did, and that there was no way at the time to find out for sure. All I knew was that it was very likely that my wife was in the other tower. I began to reflect on how, just a day or so previously, we had thought ourselves so lucky to be working together in the World Trade Center. Yet now it seemed more of a curse than a blessing.

My need to reach Mary was increasing at every step. If my cell phone didn't work, I thought, then perhaps a regular phone might. I began to look for a reentry point into the main building, and found one on the fifty-third floor. Many of my colleagues tried to convince me to keep going down the stairwell and not to enter the office. But they saw that I was set on trying to reach Mary, so they let me go.

I entered an evacuated office on the fifty-third floor just after nine o'clock. The floor was abandoned, and even though this office was thirty floors below the area of impact, there were fires and the doors had been blown out. I saw my hand shaking as I picked up the phone, and it struck me how crazy I was to be stopping. The building was burning and I was the only person in this office. Yet my urge to find out where Mary was was overwhelming. I sat down in someone's cubicle and tried to dial out, but found it impossible. I then realized after what seemed an age that this office might not dial "9" before reaching an outside extension, and so finally got a satisfactory dial tone.

My reflexes seemed to slow, and my mind was blank with grief and fear—I couldn't remember any phone numbers. Luckily, my cell phone had numbers stored in its memory. I flicked it open and pulled up some of the numbers. I tried dialing my wife's cell phone number again but was still unable to get through. I thought of others whom I might be able to call, but there was no long distance service and I was unable to get through to the part of New Jersey where Mary's family lived. I was finally able to leave a voice-mail message with Isaac Cherian, a pastor who is a good friend of my father and lives in Tappan, New York. I left a message with him and then called my cousin, who lives in Queens, New York. Normally, when I call my cousin, his wife picks up the phone and hands the receiver directly to her husband. This time I told her to stay on the line, because I didn't have time to be put through to my cousin.

"Our tower has been hit," I said. "Turn on the TV, you'll know what's going on. Tower One has been hit. I'm doing fine,"

I reassured her. "I'm getting out of the building. I have no clue where my wife is." I left my cousin's wife Mary's cell phone number, repeating it over and over until she had it written down. (As it turned out, my cousin tried to call Mary repeatedly, but couldn't get through. The only message that got to any of my relatives and friends over the next few hours was that I was on the fifty-third floor of the World Trade Center.)

My hand continued to shake as I held the receiver. "I'm going down, just call her," I said. I also asked her to call my parents in India, because I knew that whatever had happened was a major event. (My cousin was unable to reach them.) Even though I was praying that broadcasting stations would not be showing live pictures of this event around the world, I was realistic enough to know that that was precisely what they would be doing, and that the pictures would be being watched by people all over the world. I was scared that my parents would break down completely if they saw that the buildings where their son and daughter-in-law worked had been hit, so I wanted somehow to allay their fears, at least about their son.

I had just finished making the call when I heard a voice cry out behind me. "Who the hell has gone in there?" It was a police officer. On their way down, my colleagues, who were worried about me, had alerted a police officer to my presence on the fifty-third floor. "Get out of here. This is a burning building. Get out of this place." I quickly rejoined the flow of people trickling down the stairwell. As we made our way down the stairs we heard another huge explosion. It was 9:03 am.

At that moment a second plane, United Airlines Flight 175, also on its way from Boston to Los Angeles, full of fuel, and carrying sixty-five passengers, had crashed into the south tower, or Tower Two. We heard an enormous explosion, but we still had no clue as to what was going on. We just knew that something wrong was happening on the other side.

As we reached the forty-third floor we encountered firefighters, police officers, and emergency medical services personnel making their way up the stairwell, and we stepped to one side to make room for them. From that moment we begin to walk down single file to leave room for the officers going up. As they passed us, we assumed the firefighters were going to douse the flames and rescue people trapped in restrooms or other places on higher floors. None of us, even in our wildest dreams, though the building would collapse.

As the firefighters and police officers passed us we would shout encouragements to them and thank them for what they were doing. One firefighter sat down on the stairwell and said he could not go on any further. He suffered from asthma, he said, and he was having difficulty breathing. We were already out of breath from going down forty floors. I can only imagine what it was like to climb all those floors, wearing gas cylinders and all that heavy equipment in such a narrow space, all the time experiencing, as all of us were, emotional exhaustion from seeing so much destruction and worrying about our loved ones. We had no idea that these brave men were actually walking up to their deaths. People were praying for them, calling them the real heroes. "God be with you guys," we said, giving them "high-fives" and offering them water from the bottles some were carrying.

As they passed by, I kept on thinking, Don't these men have families? Don't they fear for their lives? Intellectually, I understood that these firefighters and police officers felt a sense of duty calling them to walk one way when all their instincts were to go the other way. Yet they persevered. There is not a day that goes by when I do not think of those people and the sacrifices they made for us.

Human Frailty

Throughout the entire ordeal of the plane hitting our building and my desperate attempts to call my wife, I knew that God was in control. But every time I tried to cling to a sense that everything was going to be all right, my human frailty overwhelmed my efforts to place my trust in God, and I gave up hope.

I gave up hope that God was going to take care of my wife. It seemed to me impossible that she had not made it to the south tower. And, even if she had survived whatever had happened there, I could not believe that she would have the strength to make it down the stairwell of her tower, given that she was fourteen weeks pregnant and found it difficult to walk more than a few steps, let alone scores of flights. I blamed myself, feeling as if I had forced her to go to work despite her difficult pregnancy. I found myself wishing she worked somewhere else or had called in sick that day—anything that would mean she wasn't in that building.

As we made our way down through the floors, it seemed there was a spirit of death around us. It was like a great weight of evil had cloaked the tower. You could sense it with the diesel fuel in the air, in the cascades of water from broken water pipes and sprinkler systems, the pockets of flame and smoke. It pulled on our hearts and made our feet feel leaden. As we moved into the lower floors, firefighters would direct us and help us move in a much more organized way. On some floors the firefighters would ask us to move from the stairwell to the floors, and we would walk through hallways and offices to the stairwell on the other side. This was to avoid debris or fire that was blocking the stairwells.

Everywhere we turned it seemed there were firefighters telling us to go right or left. Some of the women had taken off their shoes so that it would be easier to walk down the stairwells without tripping. "Make sure you wear your shoes when you get to the thirtieth or the fifteenth floors," they were told, "because there's glass all over." On some of the lower floors there were alarms going; the pipes had burst and sprinklers were covering the floors in water that was ankle-deep.

After what seemed an age, but was probably only fifty minutes or so after the initial explosion, we finally reached the mezzanine level of the north tower. From the mezzanine level to the lower level there was an escalator that, amazingly, was still working. I kept thinking to myself, I have to get out of the building. I am so close. I've almost made it.

The Towers Collapse

I had resolved to try and call Mary again as soon as I was out of the building. I took a few steps down the escalator and was confronted with the most appalling sight I have ever seen.

The escalator between the mezzanine and the ground floor of the north tower of the World Trade Center was situated close to a wall made of windows and doors that looked out onto the courtyard. As I looked to my left, I saw fifty to a hundred bodies scattered throughout the courtyard. They had been crushed and mutilated. Some had broken apart on impact, and there was blood everywhere. At that stage, I thought they were the bodies of people who had been in the plane that had hit our tower. However, it soon dawned on me that they were the bodies of people trapped on the floors above who had seen no way out of being burned alive except jumping to their certain deaths.

Amidst the debris I also saw the smashed shell of the globe statue that had stood between the two towers, and one of the engines from the plane. It was a far cry from the picture of the courtyard I had known only a few days previously—people happily talking and socializing, or listening to music.

When they saw the bodies lying on the ground, many people around me began sobbing uncontrollably. The firefighters and police officers kept telling us, "Don't even look on your left; just turn to your right and go down the escalator." So, keeping my face turned to my right, I made my way to the escalator and reached the lower level, where the shopping mall was.

The mall was flooded to ankle height from the burst water pipes and sprinklers. A few people fell as they tried to get out, and the officers told them to be careful. I tried several different exits but kept moving toward the south tower exit, because I thought my wife could be somewhere near there.

Finally, I found the exit for the south tower. I was thinking only of finding a pay phone of some sort and trying to reach Mary again. As I took a step out of the tower, I heard another explosion, and seconds later saw smoke and dust coming towards me from the front. My initial thought was that a car bomb had gone off in front of me. But I soon realized that it wasn't a bomb. The very building that I was standing against was collapsing. The unthinkable was happening: the south tower of the World Trade Center was coming down. It was 10:03.

As I walked toward the exit of the south tower in the lower level I had begun to feel that there was hope. I had begun to think that perhaps Mary might not have made it to the tower, or that all of us who were in the tower would get out—all of us who were still alive, that is. But as the towers began to collapse above me, all that hope vanished. I thought that I had finally reached the end. I could feel my heart pounding in my chest. All sorts of thoughts went through my head: how I so wanted to live, how I had so much I still wanted to do, how there were so many things I regretted doing and wished I could have done differently, and that now I would never be able to correct those past mistakes. I had left so many things unsaid that should have been said, and not done things that I should have done.

I cried out to God in my heart, asking why He had allowed me to walk down eighty-one flights of stairs only to let death finally catch up with me. I began to wish that I had gotten out of the building that much sooner. Why did I have to die this way and so soon? Why had I not somehow received a warning? I had only just started my life in the United States—only just started my life in any way. More than anything else I felt utterly unprepared for death. I wanted God to give me more time to be ready. I wanted more time to make sure I knew where I was going. And that was the question that came to me, as bitterness and self-pity began to fill me. It was a question that announced itself without terror or self-justification. Even as the building began to fall, I asked myself: Do you know where you are going?

Suddenly, I felt the Spirit of God speaking to my heart, telling me that with faith in God through Jesus Christ I would be resting with Him in heaven. I felt I had tried to live a life that was pleasing in God's sight, that I had lived the way the word of God charges me to live. I felt enormous gratitude for and love of Jesus and sensed the fullness of my relationship with Him. He had ordained my steps and by His blood my sins had been forgotten. Jesus, I felt assured, knew what was going on. I was in the center of God's will, and so had nothing to fear.

The peace of God suddenly gripped my heart and almost overwhelmed me, taking care of my doubts and questions, the fear and sadness that I would never see my loved ones again. I felt peace drown every other kind of emotion that I had had to that point in time. I felt calm and relaxed, because, although I thought that very shortly something was going to physically hit me and end my life on this earth, I would be going to a better place.

71

There were fifteen or twenty people in the area directly around me. Some people, seeing the dust coming toward them and thinking, as I had, that it was coming from in front of them, had run back into the building. Tragically, they were crushed by the building as it collapsed on top of them. I, however, didn't run back, but stood still, arms by my side, clutching my cell phone as a symbol of a connection to my wife. Those of us who were outside came together and began to form a huddle—each of us, men and women, piled one on top of the other. Each of us wanted the other to provide cover and protection; we wanted the sense of connection to other human beings, because we couldn't run ahead and we couldn't run back into the building. None of us wanted to be alone or lonely.

At that moment, something in my heart told me that, while I had asked where I was going and had been assured by my faith, those around me might not have asked the same question of themselves. I was filled with anxiety for them. I started crying out, "Call upon the name of the Lord and you will be saved." What I meant was not that we would all get out of the situation alive, or that only those who called upon God's name would be allowed to live. I thought we were all going to die. What I wanted was for everyone around me to have the confidence of knowing where they would end up once we all were killed. Based on our faith and our walk with the Lord, I thought, we could either end up in heaven or hell.

Even though I was speaking in my own voice, I felt the Holy Spirit speaking to everyone around me. I forgot my surroundings and started calling out Jesus' name as loudly as I could. I called upon the entire group to do the same, and we all did. We were sobbing and yelling, as the ash began to descend on our bodies.

For what seemed like five minutes, although it was probably only a few seconds, we called out Jesus' name.

At the crucial point in their lives, when death was facing them, this diverse group of men and women, of I presume many different faiths and perhaps some with no faith at all, whom I did not know and would never meet again, did not undertake any other practice, spiritual or otherwise, than calling upon Jesus. I truly believe that, in such a situation, the name of Jesus is so powerful that it overwhelms the most desperate of circumstances and calms the most terrifying of fears. Irrespective of your faith or cultural background, it is the one name under heaven and earth that can save you.

The FBI Agent

Ash and soot were falling all around us, and our huddled group found itself breaking apart as we began to peel off and scatter. Our altar of prayer splintered and I found myself about fifteen or twenty feet away by myself. There was the deafening sound of continuous explosions as the floors of the building collapsed one on top of the other, reaching a huge roar as the disintegration gathered momentum. The air was almost black with wreckage. I found myself lying face down on the ground, thinking of my wife and unborn child and my parents (now having lost both their children), reconciling myself to their and my loss, and praying that something soft would hit me and I wouldn't die a painful death!

For several minutes there was nothing but noise and soot. I then realized that nothing had hit me and felt I should get up. I opened my eyes and found myself unable to see my hand in front of my face. Everywhere I looked there was about two feet of milky white soot, obscuring every feature. The soot got into every orifice, pressing against my face, getting in my ears and nose and eyes and mouth. It began to burn my lungs, making it almost impossible for me to breathe.

Finally, the soot around me began to clear. I looked behind me to see if others were all right. To my horror, I saw another terrible scene. All the people who had been with me praying to God were lying dead on the ground, their bodies crushed by the rubble and covered in dust. Once more, my fragile humanity came to the fore and I found myself in agony, questioning God. "They just called upon Your name," I cried. "Why didn't they make it?" I felt that it was only a matter of minutes before I too died, since I was finding breathing extremely difficult. Again, I felt the Lord speaking to my heart: "Son, they made their peace with Me in their dying moments. They are resting with Me in glory."

Slowly, the atmosphere was becoming less cloudy and I could see more clearly. I looked around and found someone else alive, struggling amidst the soot that blanketed everything, sometimes it seemed to levels of twelve inches or more. I went over to the man and picked him up and saw that he was trying to say something. Once he was standing on his feet, I saw by his blue vest that he was a member of the FBI. (I have since learned that his name was Leonard Hatton.)

He looked me in the eye. "We're not going to make it," he said. "I'm having a tough time breathing and so are you, and it's going to take our lives." He took my hand.

"Are you a Christian?" I asked him.

"Yes, I am," he said.

I began to pray. "Lord God," I said, "if it is Your will that we should live, show us a way out of this place."

As I was saying this in my heart, the FBI officer began to cry out. "If anyone can hear us," he said, "if anyone can see us, we will help you get out of here." But there was silence—no moans or cries for help. Nothing.

As I was praying, I saw to my right a red flashing. It seemed to be the kind of light that came from an ambulance, and so must have been at street level. I pointed this out to the officer, and, still clutching each other's hands, we changed direction and started walking to where the light was flashing. The FBI agent had a little flashlight in his hand, but the light was making little difference; because of the white soot and dust surrounding us, the light was reflecting and diffusing all around us.

As we got closer to the light, we saw that it was indeed coming from an ambulance. Soon we could see that there were dozens of police vehicles and fire engines surrounding the ambulance, but they had all been utterly destroyed by the wreckage. The ambulance with the light was also flattened, but the front part of the ambulance was still intact, and the light flashing. I know that God had placed that light just for us, so we could find our way out of Ground Zero that morning.

We went past the ambulance and, miraculously, it was if God parted the Red Sea. The sun's rays began to penetrate the soot and smoke and we could actually see and feel our way a little better. At that moment, the FBI agent let go of my hand.

"Let's go," I said to him.

"You run ahead," he said. "I've got to go back and get more people."

So I started running ahead, even as the FBI agent turned away and started heading back in the direction of the World Trade Center. Minutes later I heard another explosion. When I turned back to look, I saw that the north tower—my tower, the one I had been working in just two hours previously—had finally fallen. I prayed to God that the FBI agent would make it out alive, because he had been heading in the direction of the north tower when he let go of my hand.

(To complete the story, and by way of another coincidence: My office was relocated to midtown Manhattan, where the FBI had also been relocated. A few days after September 11, one afternoon while I was in the elevator I started a conversation with an agent. As we talked, I shared my experience of September 11 and asked him whether anyone from the FBI had died that day. I told him that I knew the agency was busy and that they had a lot on their plates, but I wanted to know what had happened to the FBI agent who had been with me that day.

The agent took an interest in my story and escorted me to the main office, where I was interviewed. A couple of special agents asked me if they could visit my home that night and interview me further, because one FBI agent had been missing since September 11. That evening, they took down all the details of my experience, and a few days later I got a call. They told me they did not have good news: Mr. Hatton had died. I know, however, that he is resting in God's paradise today.)

The north tower fell at 10:28 a.m.

Meeting Mary

The debris from the north tower gathered momentum as it crashed to the ground and stirred up the remains of the south tower, creating a huge cloud that began to chase us through the streets as we ran from what used to be the World Trade Center. The whole area resembled a war zone, the air thick with acrid soot and smoke, and everything covered with white ash. People were crying and pointing up at the warplanes above us. They were saying that the terrorists might have penetrated our airspace, that they were dropping bombs on us, and that all skyscrapers in

Manhattan were under attack. At that point, of course, we had had no access to television or radio, and so had no idea what was going on. "Run into Chinatown," I heard a few people calling. "There aren't any skyscrapers there." So I altered my direction slightly and began to head north on Broadway.

In spite of my confidence in God's will, I could not stop my human feelings of dejection. I felt utterly without hope. Why are you running? I thought. Your wife is dead for sure. Both towers have collapsed, and the city is under attack. Where are you running? What is the point? Where are you going to hide?

At that point I saw a Manhattan city bus, parked close to the World Trade Center, and climbed in with the hope that, even though the door was open, I might get some fresh air. I was finding it almost impossible to breathe because of the soot in the air. A few other people were sitting in the bus, and one of them offered me water. I sat there, trying to get my breath back. Finally, the people on the bus, who were city workers of some kind, told me to leave the bus and go upstairs, since the dust was becoming unbearable. As I was getting out of the bus, a reporter with a microphone and a cameraman approached me.

"It seems you got out of the World Trade Center," said the reporter, sticking the microphone under my nose. "Which floor were you on?"

I was furious. "Hundreds of people have died," I answered. "My wife is also dead. Do you really need to do this?"

This reporter stood back, stunned, and dropped his microphone. That day there were many acts of heroism, but there were some who were only in search of a good story. I hope the reporter didn't ask anyone else questions like that for the rest of the day.

I began to run up Broadway again. At about 12:45 p.m. my curiosity as to what had happened overwhelmed me, and I went into a store where some young women were watching the events live on television. I was in a wretched state—in tears, still barely able to breathe properly, covered in soot and fragments of rubble and glass, and still thinking that Mary was dead. The two women began to tell me what had happened, reflecting that the kind of terror that they were so familiar with in Israel had struck the United States.

One of the young women began to remove the shattered glass from my head.

"Let me call your family for you," she offered.

"What family?" I asked her. "I have no family." I felt absolutely alone and angry at God for what had happened.

With little hope of reaching Mary, I gave the woman my cell phone, which, miraculously, I still had in my hands. Throughout the whole ordeal I had kept hold of it—not merely because I thought I might need to use it again, but because it was my only lifeline to Mary. The young woman started going through the numbers stored in the phone's address book, preparing to call the numbers using the phone she had in her store. Just as she was about to dial the first call, the cell phone sprang to life and began to ring. Immediately, she handed the phone back to me. I flipped up the lid and saw my wife's caller ID blinking at me. It couldn't be her, I thought, my heart leaping into my mouth. Someone else has got hold of her phone and is trying to reach me with the news that she is dead.

Cautiously I brought the phone to my head. "Hello?" I said.

Although the reception was extremely poor, although there was static and crackling over the phone, although I had thought it could not be possible, I heard a familiar voice that asked a question at once absurd and, for me personally, deeply moving.

"Babe, are you alive?"

Even though I knew it was Mary on the phone, I still could not quite believe it was really her. She had tried to reach me all morning on the cell phone and finally given up hope that I was alive. After I had spoken to her on the bus, she had, as on every other day, taken the E train into the World Trade Center from Port Authority. For a miraculous, unaccountable reason, her train had been delayed by about five minutes, so that it had arrived in the station at 8:50 a.m., five minutes after the first plane hit the World Trade Center.

Oblivious to the crash, Mary exited the subway. She stopped, looked up, and saw the north tower in flames and people jumping and falling from the towers. Many of them were holding hands as they threw themselves to certain death. She thought of me. There's no way my husband is going to make it out alive, she said to herself. Her mind went back to the insurance policy that I had signed. She remembered her reluctance for me to sign it, her feeling that it was too morbid. This is why he signed this insurance policy, she thought. He was supposed to go.

Mary was thinking of trying to go into the north tower to look for me when she heard the sound of the second plane hitting the south tower. At once, she was pushed and jostled by a near stampede of people, yet she somehow remained unscathed. She began to cry, not knowing what to do. She wondered whether she should run back to the towers and look for me or stay there, trying to help others and to find out if other people knew where I was. As she was crying, a young lady came up to her and asked her how she could help. Mary told her what the situation was.

This woman happened to be a Christian. She hugged Mary and said, "God is going to be with your husband." She then took Mary to an apartment in the Greenwich Village area of Manhattan and stayed with her throughout the whole ordeal, helping her make phone calls and trying to keep her calm. We never found out what that lady's name was, nor can we remember where she lived. She was truly an angel, because Mary believes that she was on the point of breaking down.

As I heard Mary's voice coming through the cell phone, my heart began to flicker with the light of hope. Our connection kept getting broken, so it was difficult for me to find out what had happened or what condition Mary was in. Yet I began to feel hopeful. Even if she has suffered some catastrophic injury, I thought, the fact that she is alive is enough for me.

I finally managed to work out that Mary was with a group of people who were on their way to New Jersey by ferry, since all bridges, tunnels, and subways were by that time closed. I told her that she should go and not wait for me, since I was still far downtown and nowhere near the ferry, which was moored at Thirty-ninth Street and Twelfth Avenue, by the Jacob Javits Center, on the Hudson River. Mary was adamant, however, that she was not going to leave Manhattan without me, and that she would meet me by the ferry. I agreed reluctantly, because I was worried that there would be a further attack and that Mary would be harmed because she was waiting for me.

I began to walk the roughly two miles from the store on Broadway to the ferry. In spite of the fact I had walked down eighty flights of stairs and already run at least a mile, a combination of adrenaline and a desperate wish to see my wife helped propel me on. It was same power that had allowed Mary to walk as far she did, even though she had had such difficulty walking over the past several days because of her pregnancy. The further north I walked, the less devastation there was, until I found myself walking through parts of the city that seemed to be almost as normal. People were emerging from restaurants after their lunch or walking to and from their offices, and they seemed neither able nor perhaps willing to grasp the magnitude of what had happened. I felt my heart breaking: How did they not know? How did they not see? How could they not in some way understand what we had all been through?

I felt that everybody was staring at me—covered in white soot as I was. A few tourists even took a picture of me, as though I was just a piece of local color to remind them of New York City. I started laughing to myself. I laughed because it was all so absurd and tragic, but I also laughed because I began to realize that, after over four hours of despair and misery, thinking I had lost Mary, my wife was alive.

I tried to hail a cab, but they were full or would not stop. I tried to hitch a lift, but only one person stopped to pick me up, and then only drove me a few blocks. As I got closer to the ferry, I began to run. Far off in the distance, I saw her, standing with a group of people in a corner. It was only then that I truly believed, to the fullest extent, that she was alive. She saw me, and my doubts vanished.

For ages we stood and hugged each other, half-believing that if we let go of each other we would somehow disappear. She was shocked at the way I looked, and we spent hours waiting for the ferry, telling each other what had happened and thanking God that we had made it out alive. As we waited there along with thousands of people attempting to get out of New York, many men and women came up to me asking me about friends and relatives who worked in the World Trade Center. They wanted to know if I knew their husband or wife or girlfriend or child who worked in the towers. They were crying and pleading with me, throwing names at me, in the vain hope that I would know. I tried as much as I could to tell them gently that there were over fifty thousand people who worked in the World Trade Center, and that I knew very few of them. My heart broke for them, not only because I could not help them, but because I knew what they going through. Ever since that day, I have been acutely aware of how desperate you become when you believe that you have lost a loved one and have no means of locating them. The need for connection had forced me to hold on to my cell phone through a building collapse and utter despair; that need had propelled me halfway across Manhattan. I understood how deep their need was, and there was nothing I could do to help them.

The Message that Changed Everything

Finally, the ferry arrived. When we reached Weehawken in New Jersey, we were decontaminated. Not only was I still covered in soot, but I had no doubt that there was still glass in my hair and toxins from the rubble all over my body. I was asked to take off my jacket and placed under some sprinklers. In addition, fire-fighters turned a high-intensity hose upon me that sprayed the glass from my hair and washed me down thoroughly. I was checked out medically and given a space suit and a yellow jacket to wear, because my clothes were utterly soaked and unwearable. We then boarded the Port Authority Trans-Hudson or PATH train, which usually takes people to and from New Jersey and New York, and which had begun to work.

When we finally reached home, at 11:30 p.m., I immediately called my parents to let them know we were alive. When the planes had hit the two towers it had been nighttime in India. My father had been watching the events unfold and had seen the buildings go down. He had lost his only daughter, and now he thought he had lost his only son—and his daughter-in-law, too. My friends and members of the church had also seen the pictures and not known what to think. For the entire night, my parents had thought that I was dead. You can imagine their joy when the phone rang and I was on the other end telling them that we were both safe. Not only did they find it hard to believe that we were both alive, but they were amazed that neither of us had a scratch on our bodies (although Mary had pulled a muscle from walking so much).

Before we went to bed that night, Mary and I knelt down at the altar near our bed and prayed. We thanked God for sparing us, and asked Him if His will was that we should go back and preach the Gospel of Jesus in the villages of India. Our future in New York, let alone the United States, seemed so uncertain. We did not know whether we had companies to work for, let alone jobs in those companies. We were asking God what He had planned for us.

The next day, early in the morning, I decided to email some of my friends and family and tell them what had happened the previous day. These were people who knew I worked in the World Trade Center in New York City and did not have my phone number. Mary and I had had a profound realization of the frailty of life, and we had been given the starkest possible reminder that we needed to know where we were going in the next life. "Do you know where you are going?" I wanted to ask my friends and relatives. "Are you at peace with yourself?"

Because I wanted to give them an opportunity to respond, I left both my cell phone number and my home phone number on the email. I had no idea that the twenty or so people to whom I sent my original message that day would in turn email that message all around the world. Before we knew it, in a matter of days, thousands of people were responding to my email or calling our telephone number, until the phone rang constantly and my email account crashed. Media from all over the world began to call, asking for my story and wanting me for interviews. As the messages of encouragement and hope began to pile up, an extraordinary new chapter in my life opened up. What happened to me after September 11 and the message that I tell everyone whom I meet are the subject of my next chapter.

5 ❦
Do You Know Where You Are Going?

YOU ARE NOW about to read the most important part of this book. It contains the heart of why I wanted to write it. My prayer is that, even as you read, the Holy Spirit will turn the searchlight on your heart and reveal to you areas in your life where you need God's help.

Since September 11 I have had the great good fortune to meet thousands of people from all walks of life. In that time, I have taken every opportunity that has come my way to pose a very important question both to individuals and to millions through the media and in my presentations. This question will be asked over and over again in many different ways through the following chapters, and I invite you to ask it of yourself as you read. That question is: Do you know where you are going?

When I ask people this question, many of them say they are not really sure of the answer. They know all about their career and their life goals; they know exactly where they are going when they retire, whether it is Florida or the Bahamas. But they become very vague when they are asked about the life to come—the eternity that happens after death. They have a vague idea that they will go somewhere, but they are not really sure where. Perhaps you are the same; perhaps you also have a fuzzy sense of heaven or hell, but you are not certain about them.

Some of you answering this question may put it another way. You may say, Well, when I'm dead I'll be dead, and I'll face whatever happens after that. I regret to say that people who say such things, who live aimlessly, are not grasping the *reality* of eternity. They are simply deluding themselves. Jesus tells a story of a very wealthy man who was consumed with the passion for amassing wealth, who thought only of enjoying himself in this life and gave no thought to eternity. But God said to him: "You fool! This very night your life will be demanded from you. Then who will get what you have prepared for yourself?" (Luke 12:20). The tragedy of this man is that while he planned so much in his short life on earth, he did not prepare for a life beyond death. This chapter will examine why we would be wise not to be like the rich man and why we should be very concerned about our life after death.

The Reality of Heaven and Hell

What I learned from my experiences on September 11 is that the question of where we are going when we die is neither vague nor academic. It is not a question that we only need to ask ourselves when we pass sixty-five or when it is convenient. It is also not a question that we can fudge or try to have both ways. We may plan every part of our life down to the ground, have all the insurance and pension plans we wish—but everything is still taking us toward eternity.

When we die, we will be confronted with another reality; and that is that heaven and hell are real places. The Bible presents us with a description of heaven and hell, and gives us a stark choice between the two. Before I explore the distinctions between heaven and hell, I wish to make clear that it is my belief that no other form of religion or faith or practice of meditation will lead us to heaven, because no spiritual leader or spiritual father other than Jesus Christ claimed to be God. Jesus claimed that He and the Father were the same (John 10:30), and that no one could go to heaven except through Him (John 14:6). He is the only God who died for our sins. On the third day after His death, Jesus rose from the dead, ascended to heaven, and sent to His disciples the Holy Spirit, which bears continual witness to the power of God in our hearts, to be with us through our spiritual journey. This message is what differentiates Jesus from all other religious leaders. All the tombs in the world carry bones or DNA strands of the great leaders. However, there is only one tomb in this world that is empty, and that is the one where Jesus was buried.

What is heaven? Heaven is a place of everlasting joy where we are finally with the Lord. The tears we have shed and the problems we have encountered on earth vanish. In heaven, the Bible says, we take on a glorified body (I Corinthians 15:43) and see our loved ones again. We will not enjoy physical relationships there, but we will know each other. This is why, for Christians, our mourning for the loss of a loved one is alleviated by the knowledge that our loved one has not disappeared forever but has simply gone ahead of us to a better place. This is why I rejoice for those people who call upon the name of the Lord in their dying moments and who are resting with Him.

Hell, on the other hand, is completely different. Some people consider hell to be a place where people of like minds can party for eternity. They are certainly correct when they understand it as eternal—for heaven *and* hell are eternal. I cannot begin to describe the horrors of hell. But there is a story in the Gospels (Luke 16:19–31) that gives a glimpse of the suffering that takes place in hell. The story concerns a rich man and his servant, Lazarus. When both die, Lazarus ends up in heaven in Abraham's bosom, while his master ends up in hell. Jesus, as He tells the story, depicts paradise and hell as far away from each other, but still visible to one another. The rich man, who is being tormented in hell and is refused comfort for his pain, cries out to Abraham in anguish: "I beg you, father, send Lazarus to my father's house, for I have five brothers. Let him warn them, so that they will not also come to this place of torment" (verses 27–28).

What the rich man understands is that, while it is too late for him, it is not too late for others. What we need to understand that Jesus Christ is always seeking us out, trying to warn us of the reality of hell and offering us the promise of heaven. This is why the need to call upon the name of Jesus is so urgent. We do not get a second opportunity. Jesus makes this very clear when He says, "One day the Lord will say, I know you not. You had an opportunity to know me, but you just turned your back on me, and I do not know you" (see Matthew 7:23). We would be wise indeed to make sure that we do not turn our back on Jesus. Eternity is too long to be wrong.

Planning for Eternity
The question now is how we make sure that we spend eternity in heaven and not in hell. In some ways, it is simply an issue of planning. In our everyday life, we spend an enormous amount of our time planning. We sit with our insurance agents or stockbrokers; we fill out our daybooks and punch in dates in our personal

organizers. Our lives are so busy, fighting against time to meet our commitments. Just out of college, we are encouraged to start planning for retirement even before we have begun to work. We plan our marriage, our education, and where we are going to retire. And some of this is sensible—I certainly was concerned about planning for my family's security when I signed the life insurance papers on September 7, 2001. Yet if we spend so much of our time planning our life on earth, a life that is so short, how much more planning should we do, how many more resources, and how much more energy should we devote to eternity?

Another reason we need to ask ourselves the question, Do you know where you are going? is that death is the one certain thing in this uncertain world. Ever since Adam and Eve sinned in the Garden of Eden, death has been our legacy from cradle to grave—an inescapable fact for every man and woman. As the Bible says, "The last enemy to be destroyed is death" (I Corinthians 15:26).

It is worth dwelling on the fact of death, because we too often push it out of our minds. You could be the richest or the poorest individual on earth, you could be in New York or on the streets of Calcutta, you could be from China, or South America, or Africa. It does not matter. For every one of us there will come a time when death will knock on our door. My sister was barely seven years old when it happened to her. For some people the moment comes when they are twenty-five, or forty-five, seventy, or ninety. Some may reach a hundred years of age or more. But at the end of it all, death is still there. When I worked in the World Trade Center, I used to brush shoulders with some of the richest people in the world, people who had made it big in the stock market and in technology. On Fridays, I would see people in their golf T-shirts talking about their weekend plans, their cars and yachts and houses. But none of them could take their money or stocks or fast cars with them when they died that day. September 11 has taught me that everything we hold onto could be gone in a day and that when death knocks at the door, what stares us in the face is our destiny.

At that moment, it is too late to decide to do something about our life. It is too late to try to repair the damage we have done. No amount of good work will change the essential issue of whether you have committed yourself to Christ or not. My sister lived her life committing herself to Christ and died with Jesus' name on her lips. The people who huddled with me as the south tower collapsed around us called upon Jesus at the moment of their deaths. Jesus heard my sister's cries and the cries of those with me near the south tower, and they are now in heaven. But for those who are not ready to welcome Him into their heart, even at the moment of destiny, there is a different fate.

Even though we think we can anticipate or postpone our deaths, we are wrong: the exact time we are to depart this world is in God's hands. I do not know when I will die. On September 11, God ordained that it was not my time to die, even though I felt many times that I was indeed about to lose my life. My *belief* in the saving grace of Jesus Christ was not what kept me alive. What kept me alive was the grace of God. His grace forced me to acknowledge His presence when, in my human frailty, I had lost hope or felt everything was lost. He bathed me in the warmth of His love and called upon me to help those in the direst situation that any of us can face—when we face our destiny and have not given ourselves over fully to the love of God. This was my mission in the moments when the towers began to fall and I asked the people around me to call upon Jesus' name, and it is my mission for everyone I meet, and for you reading this book.

The morning of September 11, 2001, was not my time to go. But I do not take pride in my survival. I am neither a better Christian nor worthier a person than those who died. Rather, I see the situation as if we were all people waiting in line for a bus. The bus came along and there were only twenty-five seats on board, and fifty people waiting. Twenty-five people got on, and those who remained wait for the next bus to take them to their destination. Whether we were on this bus or will be on the one after that, and so on, the buses *will* come and we will all eventually climb on.

I believe that God kept me alive in this world to share the message of Jesus Christ, because time is running out. I believe that the Second Coming of Jesus Christ is upon us. Like my death, I do not know when it will happen, because no one knows. However, events around us only show that something is occurring; the news is too discouraging from various parts of the world for there not to be hints of the times to come. This puts into perspective the lives of those who died and those of us who are still alive. As the Bible says, we are surrounded by a cloud of witnesses (Hebrews 12:1), godly people who are looking down upon us, encouraging us to persevere in our faith. September 11 greatly added to those witnesses, and we are blessed by that.

In the next chapter I want to explore in more detail how we turn our lives over to Christ. For I want to emphasize that Christianity offers a message of hope and not despair. Christianity is unique in the sense that it talks not about the past, but the future, and lays out a simple plan for that future. Christianity is encouraging us to buy a ticket to heaven. If you want to go from New York to Seattle, you buy a ticket from an airline or a travel agent. If you want to go to heaven, your ticket is your acceptance of the

6 🌿
Accepting the Lord

A N EXAMPLE OF what can happen if you ask yourself, Do you know where you are going? may be found in the story of Miguel Roman. Soon after I sent out the email about what happened to Mary and me on September 11, I received a call late one Friday afternoon from Miguel, a young man who lived in downtown Chicago. He seemed agitated.

"Is this the Sujo that sent out this email?" he asked. "Because my wife just got this email, and she forwarded it to me."

I told Miguel that, yes indeed, I was *that* Sujo, and explained that it was possible that a person had forwarded the message on to his wife from someone else who had been sent the email by one of my friends or relatives. By that time, we were receiving so many emails and phone calls that it was impossible to know through how many channels my initial email had been circulated.

"What's your background?" he asked suspiciously.

Initially, I wasn't sure what he meant. However, I soon realized that he was asking me which religion I professed.

"Ever since I read your email," he continued, "with that short challenge, 'Do you know where you are going?' something's been happening in my heart."

I asked him what his religious background was.

"I'm not really sure," he replied. "Although I was raised in a Catholic home, I've never been in a church. So I don't know where I stand before God."

"Miguel," I said. "It is not an accident that you called me. It was God's appointment in your life."

At that moment he began crying. "I really want to live for God," he said. "You asked this question in your email, 'Do you know where you are going?' And if I were to put myself in your shoes, I wouldn't know where I am going, because I don't have that faith. And I'm really not sure where I am going. But I want to have the same peace that you enjoy, so tell me what I should do."

I felt very excited at what I was hearing and asked Mary to start praying, even as I was talking on the phone. I told Miguel that what he had to do was easy. "Give me five minutes over the phone," I said, "just to explain the message of Jesus Christ. Let me share the love of the Lord on the phone with you."

I told him that God was constantly trying to reach us with His love. Many people go through life thinking that it's the other way around—that we have to strive to reach God. But, I continued, this is hopeless, because we are too weak. I told him that all he had to do was allow God into his heart. "If you call upon His name you will have this peace," I said. "And you can have the same peace that I enjoy if you just say a simple prayer and call out to God with a humble heart, and mean it."

For five minutes I shared the message of Jesus Christ—how God came down from Heaven and through the life, death, and resurrection of His Son, Jesus Christ, He took upon Himself the sins of the world and gave us everlasting life. I told him that through believing in the bodily resurrection of Jesus Christ, by turning over our sins to Him and worshiping Him, we are promised a life in heaven, far from the terrors of this world.

As I continued to share this message, Miguel told me that he felt a sense of peace coming upon him. I then asked him to repeat after me a prayer of forgiveness and of welcoming the Lord into his heart. This he did. He began to cry like a little child.

"I feel a sense of peace coming upon my life," he said, "so much peace. I feel something has entered my heart. I feel just like a child."

"That's the presence of God," I told him. "That's the Holy Spirit doing new work in your life."

"Sujo," Miguel said, "I want to follow the same God that you follow. I don't understand much about Christianity, but I hear that there are a lot of cults or other kinds of teaching in Christianity. I want to make sure I serve the same God you do."

The force of his statement struck me. For a new Christian, especially someone who has no sense of the history or cultural traditions of Christianity yet is surrounded by different churches, denominations, and sub-denominations, it is very hard to know where to turn. Every denomination proclaims that it is the correct version of the faith, and seeks to undermine other parts of the larger Church by competing for membership in a cutthroat campaign that would put Wall Street to shame. For the newly converted, the doctrinal differences between Episcopalians, Baptists, Presbyterians, and Pentecostals are unimportant. They are experiencing the first fruits of a personal relationship with

Jesus, one that it is in the process of transforming their lives. They need to feel welcomed within a nurturing community that can help them through the tough times and start them successfully on the hard road of being a practicing Christian.

"Miguel," I replied. "What is your doubt that you should ask me this question?"

"I want to ask you this simple question," he said. "Do you think Billy Graham is OK? Do you serve the same God as Billy Graham?"

"Miguel," I said, laughing with joy. "Billy Graham is the greatest man of God to have lived in our times. Yes, Billy Graham is OK."

I was concerned that Miguel take the opportunity to go to a church that Sunday. However, because the next day was Saturday, I knew that I wouldn't be able to call anyone in Chicago to find a church where Miguel could go. I had hoped to call my pastor in Chicago and ask him to pick Miguel up and take him to this church, but logistical difficulties made that impossible.

"I am in New York, and you are in Chicago," I told him. "I don't think there's much I can do for you here. You are a new Christian; you need to be rooted in the word of God. You need to learn more about the word of God. You must go to a church." He told me there was an evangelical church in his neighborhood and I advised him to go. "When you go to this church," I said, "make sure you arrive a little early. Please share your story with the pastor, so he can disciple you and help you out."

Early on Sunday morning Miguel and his wife arrived at church—the first church he had been to in his entire life. He shared his story with the pastor, who was delighted and told him that he would like Miguel to talk to the congregation about his experience. So, during the service, Miguel stood up and did exactly that. After hearing the story of how her husband had been moved by the email message to give himself to God, Miguel's wife, who was also in church for the very first time, accepted the Lord.

Often during the next few weeks, Miguel would call to tell me what was happening in his life. Each week there would be a new blessing. The Sunday after he had told his story and his wife had given herself to the Lord, he had taken his sister to the same church and she had dedicated herself to God. The very next week Miguel took his brother to church, and he was also saved. Following that, the family went to visit Miguel's other brother in jail. In prison, Miguel shared his story and told his brother how God had been working in his life, and his brother accepted the Lord.

For me this story confirms not only the extraordinary power of the Internet, but also how deeply all of us need to answer the question of where we are going. It was a question that resonated so deeply with Miguel that it spoke to the very core of his being. It was a question that demanded to be answered. I was blessed to be able to share with him my answer to that question, which allowed him to open himself to God's peace and to share that openness with the members of his family. Miguel's story showed me how powerful is God's peace and how great is the possibility of transformation when you call upon the name of Jesus. I will talk about more lessons I gathered from Miguel's experience later on in the book.

The Impact of Jesus

The answer to Miguel's fundamental question was Jesus Christ. The powerful story of Jesus Christ has been told for two thousand years all over the world. In the Bible, Jesus charges his disciples with the following commandment: "Therefore go and make disciples of all nations, baptizing them in the name of the Father and of the Son and of the Holy Spirit, and teaching them to obey everything I have commanded you" (Matthew 28:19–20). Millions have answered that call and have gone to the farthest ends of the earth with the light of Jesus Christ burning within them. One of them came to Kerala and began the process that led to my family's discovery of Jesus Christ; thousands have died bearing witness to His name—including many on September 11. I hope the light of Jesus Christ can come to you reading this book as well.

Historian Philip Schaff has described the overwhelming influence that Jesus has had on world history and culture in the following way:

> *This Jesus of Nazareth, without money and arms, conquered more millions than Alexander, Caesar, Mohammed, and Napoleon; without science...he shed more light on things human and divine than all philosophers and scholars combined; without the eloquence of schools, he spoke such words of life as were never spoken before or since, and produced effects which lie beyond the reach of orator or poet; without writing a single line, he set more pens in motion, and furnished themes for more sermons, orations, discussions, learned volumes, works of art, and songs of praise than the whole army of great men of ancient and modern times.*

What is it about Jesus Christ that compels such allegiance and such expressions of devotion? What does it mean to welcome Jesus into our heart and be "born again?" How do we do what Miguel Roman did—decide to make that decision about our lives and ask ourselves the toughest question of all: Do you know where you are going? The next section of this chapter attempts to answer these questions.

The Love and Compassion of Jesus Christ

As I have learned over and over again since September 11, in talking with people throughout the United States, all people carry with them some tragedy, whether big and small, that has affected them or those they love. Life contains enormous pain and suffering, and sometimes it seems that everything is utterly hopeless. My experience on September 11 shows that despair is always threatening to overwhelm us. However, no matter what we are going through there is one person who understands our experience, and that is Jesus Christ. We might hide our pain in front of our spouse, or wear a mask in church and pretend that all is well. But inside us we feel a void—a void that cannot be filled by anything but the peace of God and Jesus Himself.

This void accompanies us as we go through this world. Some of us try meditation to fill it. Others pursue the world's pleasures, in drugs or promiscuous sex. We think we will somehow get rid of the emptiness, the inner longing that makes us search. But what those who seek to fill the void with things of this world do not understand is that God Himself created the void in our hearts so He could live there. The Bible teaches us that He dwells in our hearts through faith (see Ephesians 3:17). Because the body is the temple of God, the void cannot be filled by anything else.

This is not to suggest that we should not search for spiritual fulfillment; it is that we spend our lives looking in the wrong places to find it. God is constantly seeking us out, showing us His presence in the world. He is wooing us, serenading our souls. He is doing this even as you are reading this book. On September 11, He was with the firefighters who struggled up the stairs and the FBI agent who went to rescue more people and died in the attempt. He was there when my colleagues tried to reassure me that my wife was not dead. He was with the woman who came and helped Mary in her distress. He was with the two young Jewish women who offered to help me make contact with my family and took glass from my hair. He was with Miguel when he picked up the phone. God is always trying to make an appointment with our souls, to make us listen to the message of Jesus Christ.

So, to answer one of the questions I began this section with, the way we can have the grace of Jesus Christ in our lives is to invite Him into our hearts, and to do so with all humility. We need to say, "God, in my own strength I cannot do it. I want you in my heart. Cleanse me from my sins with your blood."

By asking the blood of Jesus to cleanse us, we are committing to being born again. The phrase "born again" is used a lot in Christian circles. But what does it mean? The phrase comes from an episode in the Bible when a young man came to Jesus by night for counsel. Jesus said to him, "I tell you the truth, no one can see the kingdom of God unless he is born again" (John 3:3). Being born again means that the old us has passed away and the new us has been born. The prayer to be born again will cost us a lot, because we will be challenged not to go back to our old lifestyle and do the things we used to do. It is a commitment to fighting the old temptations or habits (drugs, sexual promiscuity, crime, etc.) that dragged us away from God.

This commitment to God is called being "born again" not simply because one feels like a new person, as if the slate, as it were, has been washed clean and we can start again. It is because we are like a baby in the arms of God. When a baby is born it feeds on the mother's milk, and that is all it knows. That milk for a Christian is the word of God. When you are a new Christian, you commit your life to the Lord. You do not understand much about the mysteries of the spirit and the challenge of the Christian life. Because God has given us the free will to accept Him or reject Him, all He can do is cause a tug in our heart to let us know how much He wants us and loves us. It is up to us whether we want to respond or not.

The tug that draws us to God, that worked in Miguel as he was on the phone, is the Holy Spirit. Someone in his own strength seeking God cannot do anything without the anointing presence of the Holy Spirit. It is the Holy Spirit that puts a searchlight on our hearts and reveals to us the inner sense of who we are that only we know. It is the Holy Spirit that gives us the strength to ask for help in taking away the sins we have been battling with. When people sin, they think they are getting pleasure. But how long is that pleasure? If you believe that two shots of whiskey is enough for you to drown your sorrow, what happens when you've finished the bottle? When you get up the next morning, have you forgotten your problems? People look for answers in temporary pleasures that lead to the destruction not only of our body but of our soul. With God in our hearts we are encouraged to press on and claim the strength we need to overcome the temptation.

Being born again means truly and completely acknowledging our weakness and accepting the love of God—a love so great that God allowed Himself to suffer and die in extreme pain on the Cross, took upon Himself the sins of all humanity, and then offered us the promise of eternal life through the mystery of His resurrection. Being born again is about believing that God came down to earth to die for and redeem *your* sins—that He took *your* place and paid the debt that He did not owe. It is about acknowledging the free gift that is salvation. And this can be accomplished simply by asking Jesus to come and live in your heart and to get rid of all the junk that is in it at the moment.

Jesus Himself showed us an example of being born again when he was baptized. His cousin, John the Baptist, was in the River Jordan when Jesus approached to be baptized (Matthew 3:13). John the Baptist said, "Look, the Lamb of God, who takes away the sin of the world!" (John 1:29). I sometimes wonder what was running through John the Baptist's mind—when the redeemer of our sins asked to be baptized by him! John the Baptist knew that he was appointed as the forerunner to Jesus. The Bible tells us he was crying out in the wilderness, saying, "I baptize you with water for repentance. But after me will come one who is more powerful than I, whose sandals I am not fit to carry. He will baptize you with the Holy Spirit and with fire" (Matthew 3:11).

By undergoing a baptism, just as all new Christians undergo the baptism, Jesus shows us the practical message of the Gospel—humility. Once Jesus is baptized, He begins His ministry; and this is what He asks of all Christians once they have been born again through knowledge of Him: "Therefore go and make disciples of all nations, baptizing them in the name of the Father and of the Son and of the Holy Spirit" (Matthew 28:19). So baptism is a sign to the world and to yourself, a strengthening of that commitment you made the first time when you came to the Lord and were born again.

Being born again does not mean that all we wish for will come true. As I learned with my sister and the people around me who died when the towers fell, calling upon the name of Jesus does not mean that your physical life will be spared. Instead, as I have pointed out frequently in this book, this life is a transitory, fragile thing. It is short and often painful. What calling upon the name of Jesus means, what being born again means, is that our eternal life is saved.

What, we may ask, is the nature of the Christian life? What can Miguel Roman look forward to? I will examine this in the next section.

The Christian Life

The first time the word "Christian" is used in the Bible is of people in Antioch in Asia Minor (Acts 11:26). They were called Christians because they followed the teachings of Jesus. In other words, they were living a Christ-like life. In this section I will examine what it means to live a Christ-like life, to be a practicing Christian.

The idea of being born again and being a Christian has been misunderstood or misrepresented. It does not mean, as Miguel Roman feared it would, that you practice mysterious or strange rituals. It has nothing to do with traditions or culture or your name. It is not about what people say or the rules that people feel they can apply to the word of God. Some think their good works will get them to heaven. Some think their mere attendance in church or being a member of a church will get them to heaven. Our good works and being a member of a church or being baptized into the faith are all important. But they will not get you into heaven. What matters is having a personal relationship with Jesus Christ.

God has made us in His likeness and has blessed us with an opportunity to know Him. At the heart of Christianity is that connection, and the mystery of faith, such as it is, lies in the knowledge that God is the author and finisher of our faith. If we place our life in God, there is nothing for us to fear about the future. If I know Jesus, that is all I need to care about. Other things will fall into place.

The Good News of Jesus Christ as expressed in the Gospels in the New Testament of the Bible is eminently practical. It offers wisdom that can apply to day-to-day living. This is why I emphasize that Christianity is not a religion of traditions and rituals. Christianity means living a Christ-like life and emulating His goodness. It means having a daily conversation with God, a relationship that is an everyday experience of walking with Him and having a fellowship with Jesus as your friend. A personal relationship with Jesus is your ticket to heaven.

At times in our lives, there are situations we experience that we cannot share even with the best of our friends, our spouse, or even mentors or pastors. When you have a relationship with Jesus, however, you can talk to God like a friend and share your problems with Him. That is the relationship I enjoy. When I have terrible moments—such as September 11, when I felt absolutely alone—I talk to God, or cry out to Him or argue with Him and debate with Him, because He is my friend. I talk to Him as if He were a normal person, when I am sitting on the bus or driving or taking a walk. And that is what prayer is—talking to God. We all need to aspire to that walk and relationship with God.

If we can attain that relationship, then the words of the Bible become true for us: "Let the peace of Christ rule in your hearts" (Colossians 3:15). That peace, which is what Miguel Roman experienced, is the presence of God in our heart. With the presence of God in your heart, when you pass a bar and are tempted to go in and drink or you are about to stray from your marriage vows, your connection with Him will help you fight that temptation. This is how the Gospel is practical.

Yet we shouldn't expect this to happen easily. To continue the metaphor I discussed earlier: as a baby we begin our Christian lives, knowing little. Then, as we get deeper and deeper into the word of God and learn from it, we develop a daily prayer life, a life where we read the word of God, and try to live a Christ-like life. That is what Christianity is all about, living like Christ. The Bible tells us that Christ Himself was tempted (Matthew 4) and showed us a unique way for us to fight temptation.

The Bible tells us "the wages of sin is death" (Romans 6:23). God is the God of love, and He is patient. But he is also the God of justice. Although God wants fellowship with us because He is holy, our sin and His holiness are incompatible. By His grace and through the sacrifice of His blood, we are cleansed of our sins and become holy. Only then can we approach His presence. Sin in our heart, however, keeps us separate.

My sister's death showed me that, as Jesus knew, it is the faith of children that most completely approximates what Jesus meant by faith. The child who gave money on his birthday in the story that Ray Boltz told expressed faith. It was, as Mark Buntain said, evident in the child who was chosen to help feed the five thousand people. Jesus asked His disciples not to hinder the children from approaching him. Jesus said, "Let the little children come to me, and do not hinder them, for the kingdom of heaven belongs to such as these" (Matthew 19:14). It is to children that things that are hidden from adults are revealed (Matthew 11:25). Jesus said, "I tell you the truth, unless you change and become like little children, you will never enter the kingdom of heaven" (Matthew 18:3).

What is meant by the faith of children is not a naïve, ignorant faith, but one that is trusting and humble—neither self-serving nor overly pleased with itself. A Christ-like life is a life of humility, compassion, and abundant love. Let us examine what we mean by abundance and humility.

Abundance and Humility

Christianity is a life where God pours out His blessings on you abundantly, and you have more abundant life, although not necessarily of the material kind. The fisherfolk my youth group visited in Orissa, India were extremely poor in terms of material possessions, but they had abundance because the joy of Jesus Christ was in their hearts. They knew they were only temporary citizens of this world, if only because so many of them each morning set sail on the dangerous waters of the Bay of Bengal. Humility is about acknowledging how few talents we have. If someone believes that God is using him just because of who he is, he is a fool, because it is the spirit of God that works in our hearts and minds. The greatest example of humility is Mother Teresa, who had no possessions and was of tiny stature, and yet had enormous power for good. Greatness should only be measured by what you have in your heart.

A Christ-like life calls us to take up a life of humility, because as the Bible says, in the end, "the last will be first, and the first will be last" (Matthew 20:16). Humility means embracing the spirit of Jesus, which in turn means sharing what we have. Now Jesus shared His life, which in a physical sense it is difficult for us to do, although the firefighters and the FBI agent on September 11 did just that in giving their lives for others. They truly lived Jesus' maxim: "Greater love has no one than this, that he lay down his life for his friends" (John 15:13). If we are not called on to give our lives, then we need to share our lives in other ways—by preaching the Gospel, by giving to those who have less, and by emulating Christ in all the ways we can.

At times we can be self-satisfied about our closeness to God. At such moments, pride can overwhelm us, as it has so many, and bring about our downfall. When you feel you are open to the sin of pride, you should always remind yourself of where you came from. You should remember just how empty and, literally, hopeless your life was before you met the Lord. God in His mercy gave you an opportunity to respond to His love. He wooed you and you responded to His serenade. Throughout your life, from your cradle onward, God was always calling you. Even though you were sinful, He touched you with His love, which is why you enjoy His peace.

Had it not been for that courtship by God, had it not been for His strength, even now, we would be nothing. We might ask of God, as the Psalmist did, "What is man that you are mindful of him?" (Psalm 8:4). As the Psalmist also says, "As for man, his days are like grass, he flourishes like a flower of the field; the wind blows over it and it is gone, and its place remembers it no more" (Psalm 103:15–16). If you think you are able to accomplish something or feel you are someone without God you are a fool, because it is the Lord who lifts up men and women. One of my favorite verses in the Bible comes from the First Book of Samuel (2:8): "He raises the poor from the dust and lifts the needy from the ash heap; he seats them with princes and has them inherit a throne of honor. For the foundations of the earth are the Lord's; upon them he has set the world." That speaks volumes about humility.

A story that illustrates for me humility and the abiding love of God for all people happened to me after one of my engagements after September 11. Soon after the email went out, I was called by the Christian Broadcasting Network's 700 Club program for an interview. This was an honor and a blessing for me. The senior producer of the program, Cheryl Wilcox, and a camera crew came to my house and filmed me telling my story. The day was a taxing one. The President of the United States was in New York City, and F-16 fighters were flying over the city as precaution and protection. It meant that Cheryl, who was fasting that day, had to stop the filming when the planes flew over. When the program went on the air, Rev. Dr. Pat Robertson, the host of the show, gave an altar call immediately after I finished speaking, asking people to call up and make their pledge to God.

A few days after the show aired, Cheryl called me on the telephone. "Sujo," she said. "You will not believe what has happened. Four hundred and twenty-nine people called and accepted the Lord, and over a thousand people called to know more about Jesus." She told me that was the best response they had received in years. That news made me feel as though God had a plan for my life. It made me feel as though there was something special that God wished to communicate through me, and gave me encouragement to continue.

I also received requests to speak from all over the United States. On one of those engagements I was in Jacksonville, Florida, where I had just finished speaking at the Thanksgiving Service at First Baptist Church. It is one of the largest churches in the country, with over ten thousand members. I felt truly blessed to be able to speak there and share my story. The Saturday morning after speaking I was checking out of my hotel to go back to New Jersey when apparently something slipped out of my pocket. A lady behind me said, "Sir, you have dropped something."

I turned around and saw that my pen had fallen on the floor. I looked up to thank the lady and saw that she was a cleaning woman, who was vacuuming the corridor, and that she was wearing a veil. Something in my heart told me that I should ask where she was from, since in the months after September 11 I had, like many others, become more aware of cultural symbols such as the veil as we saw pictures of women in Afghanistan wearing the *burqa*.

Although her English was broken, the lady told me she was from Afghanistan. For some reason, her response was a shock. At that time, American and allied forces were engaged in a military campaign in Afghanistan, trying to root out Al-Qaeda terrorists, who were responsible for the attacks on September 11, and the remnants of the Taliban government that had supported them. There was something shocking, almost intimidating, about someone from Afghanistan being in Jacksonville, Florida. Many people in the United States were finding out for the first time where Afghanistan was and learning about the terrible conditions for women in that country. Even to those of us who grew up in closer geographic proximity to Afghanistan, it remained a remote and mysterious country. Yet, here was an Afghan, vacuuming the corridor of a hotel in Jacksonville, Florida, and talking to me.

I asked the lady whether she had family in Florida, and she told me that she had a husband and children in the States. I then asked her whether she had family in Afghanistan, wondering how they were faring now and how they had survived under the oppressive Taliban regime.

She said that she did have family in Afghanistan.

"How are they doing?" I asked.

She began to break down. "The Taliban has killed my father and my brothers," she said. "They were beheaded."

I had been on the 700 Club and had just come from speaking to ten thousand people; I was feeling quite pleased with myself for speaking the Gospel of the Lord. Yet here was a study in humility—a woman who had lost her father and brothers in such a cruel manner. Beyond the pictures on television and the nightly

109

reports of terrorists being rounded up, this woman brought back to me the human dimension of suffering that I saw on September 11. It made meaningful for me the United States' efforts to root out the Taliban and Al-Qaeda in Afghanistan.

I asked the woman whether I could pray for her, and she said that I could. I am sure she understood I was a Christian, and I knew she was a Muslim, yet we began to pray together.

"God," I said. "I pray that You will fill this woman with Your peace." It was all I could say, because there was nothing for me to offer her. I prayed for peace for her family and for the protection for her loved ones left in Afghanistan. When I had finished praying, I opened my eyes and saw this lady still had her eyes closed and was weeping quietly. I began to talk to her, to let her know as gently as I could that I had stopped praying. Finally, I said, "God be with you," and left.

As I got on my flight heading back to New Jersey I reflected on what had happened and felt God speak to my heart. He made me realize that there was so much hurt in the world—that no matter whether it was the horrific experiences I and others had seen and undergone on September 11 or what this woman's family had been through in Afghanistan, everyone had a story to tell. It made me realize that behind the thousands of people who had heard me speak, there were individuals who were going through real struggles in their lives, and that reaching them with the message of love and compassion of Jesus Christ was as important as the kind of mass rallies I had begun to address.

Pressing on in the Christian Life

Having a daily relationship with Jesus Christ and trying to live a Christ-like life is hard, especially in today's world, where there are so many distractions, temptations, and potentialities for despair.

Being a practicing Christian is a life of struggles where you constantly fail. As I found out on September 11, human beings are as frail as they are resilient, as prone to despair as to hope. I was confronted with my death and the despair at losing my wife many times that day, but I kept on. This is what Mark Buntain of the Assemblies of God Church in India would always tell us: Press on. God did not intend that Christians had to be superhuman—quite the reverse. God wants us to recognize how weak we are. What we have to do is to call upon God, to say, "God, in my own strength I cannot do it." Our weakness is made strong through His strength in our lives.

As a new Christian, coming to the Lord does not mean the end of your problems, that you will have an untroubled sleep and a bright halo on your head. In fact, the Devil will tempt you, as he did Jesus, that much more assiduously. This time, however, you will have the strength to fight. The more rooted you are in the word of God, the more rooted you get in the promises of God to be with you when you are tempted. This is why Christians should read the Bible, to cultivate that rootedness and protection against temptation. Reading the Bible allows the Christian to renew his or her mind and spirit with the things of God and want to learn more. My moral standard and my banner is the word of God. So I read the Bible for answers and encourage every Christian to do the same. The Bible can provide a grounding point for us to ascertain how truthful are those who speak to us and how truthful are the things we read. Any time you hear someone speaking, whether at a Sunday morning service or elsewhere, check in with the Bible and see how consistent that message is with the word of God.

When you read the Bible you see how God spoke to His people, the Israelites, through different prophets. Then God Himself came down to earth in the shape of Jesus. When God wanted to connect again with His people, He knew that there was no way to win His people back unless He sent His son. So God Himself came down in the shape of Jesus and died for our sins, because the justice of God demanded a price, and the only price that could match the scale of the sacrifice was the blood of God. Through that sacrifice the price has been won, and has opened up a way for us to connect with God. Even after He left, Jesus said, "I go, but I send you the comforter, I send you the Holy Spirit" (see John 14:26). And the Holy Spirit encourages us and stays with us, helping us to press on.

At the end of any service I speak at, when I do an altar call, I always ask people not to be swayed by where they are sitting or who is next to them. They may be thinking what I was thinking when I put my hand up and made a commitment to God when I was twelve years old because I saw some of my contemporaries doing the same. But there is no use pretending: God knows you don't mean it.

God is not a bully. If He wanted you to believe in Him against your will, He could do it; He has the power. But He has given us free will, the chance to decide whether we want to respond to the Lord or not. The Bible teaches us two aspects of God's will that are relevant for our salvation. These are His perfect will and His permissive will (see Matthew 7:21 and Luke 7:30). God's perfect will is that no one should die and we should all repent of our sins (see 2 Peter 3:9). This is what God desires. Yet His permissive will allows those who choose to remain unsaved to be so. God will not force or coerce anyone to accept Jesus Christ.

As I suggested earlier, the life of Christ is about abundance and joy. Christians can have fun! It is not that, as a Christian, you have to walk around with a gloomy face or a frown. The word of God says, "the joy of the Lord is your strength" (Nehemiah 8:10).

This means that we can have fullness of joy in God. Being a Christian also means that we make mistakes. We are, after all, human, and we all sin. God loves you not because of your talents but in spite of your lack of them. He loves you because of who you are. He doesn't hate the sinner, He hates the sin. That's the differentiation He makes.

In all our tribulations and mistakes, if we call upon Jesus, the Holy Spirit dwells in our hearts and reveals the ways we are moving away from God. This is what happens in my life. Every time I fall, I get up, because I know that God is a forgiving God and I ask Him for His forgiveness. Christianity is not a short sprint, where you get the baton and finish the race. It's a long marathon, which you run with perseverance and with the support of His grace.

In the next chapter, I discuss the obligations of living a Christlike life and living with abundance.

7 🦎

The Challenge of Being a Christian

T HROUGHOUT THE BIBLE, God uses ordinary people for His message. In spreading the Gospel God used twelve simple people, many of them fishermen, to take this Gospel of the Lord all over the world. If he had wanted scholars or the highly educated He would have gone to the Pharisees or Sadducees, who were very learned men of God, and used them. Instead, He looked into the hearts of these poor fishermen, just as He looks into the hearts of the fishermen of Orissa today. Jesus said, "Blessed are you who are poor, for yours is the kingdom of God" (Luke 6:20). God's love is an unconditional love, called *agape*, which means that He loves you no matter who you are, where you come from, or what your color is. He loves me, a Christian, as He loves a Muslim or a Hindu, the same way, because all are His children. He gives us all an opportunity to respond to His *agape*.

In this chapter I would like to present a challenge to all new Christians. Jesus wants us to share our good news and the talents we possess—just like Miguel Roman did with his family. If we simply keep these gifts to ourselves, we will have to give an account of what we did not do. God has placed us in different circumstances on this planet to do what we can with what we can. And we need to acknowledge humbly that everything comes from God. We need to say, "God, all I am is because of Your presence and Your spirit working in my life. My flesh is weak. But because You are working in my life, I am able to accomplish great things." Jesus knows that in His name we can do greater things. The challenge for us as Christians is not to be passive about our faith. It is not to be self-satisfied that we are superior because somehow we know the Lord and others do not. We and we alone are responsible for the decisions we make, and one day, when we stand before God, we will have to give an account of our time.

There is a story about a man who died and went to heaven, and the angel took him to a large warehouse. On the way he passed a lot of mansions. As he passed by them, the man thought, "That could be my mansion that Christ was talking about. But why is he taking me to this warehouse?" He saw stacks and shelves with little boxes on them. "These gifts could be for me," he said to himself. "But why so many gifts? I could not possibly handle them." So he asked the angel, "What is this warehouse?"

The angel replied, "Oh, I just wanted to show you something. These are all the gifts you could have had if only you had asked for them while you were on earth." And the man fell on his face and said, "I wanted these gifts, but I thought that I had to do everything myself. I needed the gifts, but I did not know how to get them. I thought God didn't have an answer."

What this story tells us is that God could have used this man in a much more powerful way, and the man could have enjoyed more blessings from God, if only he had asked for them. He was a holy man, he lived a holy life, and he did things for God. But he could have done so much more had he just attended to God and spent more time on his knees praying, "God, use me, or bless me with these gifts." We would be wise to be unlike the man who visited the warehouse and did not call upon the many gifts that God had ready for us.

Knowing the Lord is a joy that transforms our lives. As Miguel Roman discovered, it is a joy that cannot be contained but must be communicated. Miguel found a peace in his life and wished to tell all those he loved about it. His joy communicated itself, and his wife, sister, and two brothers were saved. The joy that comes from knowing God and having a personal relationship with Jesus Christ means reaching out to those who do not have a relationship and asking them to call upon His name so they might know the Kingdom of God. Miguel loved his family enough to know that it was not enough that they should be pleased he had found peace. He needed to know that they too would share his peace and share with him the hope of an everlasting life in paradise.

As Christians we are called upon to reach out to those in distress and give them the possibility of eternal life through calling on the name of Jesus. It grieves me deeply to know that there were those who died on September 11, as there are millions who die each day throughout the world, who do not know the saving grace of Jesus Christ.

The calling of the Christian is to work for the souls of human beings much as the notion of individual liberty in the United States does for the lives of its citizens. We need to provide every resource, spend every moment, and work with all our effort not merely to provide someone with peace in this life, but to work for their salvation in the next. It is a huge and difficult task, but we must press on. We will be assailed by doubt, we will be plagued by temptation. The Devil is everywhere present, sowing the seeds of discord, working to undermine our efforts to show God's love for the world and for every single human being. But we must press on, offering the great good news that Jesus Christ died for us, is risen again in our hearts, and awaits us in heaven with all those who have gone before us.

The Transformation of Reaching Out

Reaching out to others is a blessing that works both ways. Both Miguel Roman and the Afghan lady had been opened by the grace of God to be touched on an individual level. Their tears had allowed them a breakthrough. But what was also significant was that I too had been blessed by their openness, I had been transformed by the acknowledgment of their suffering. I had been made profoundly aware that Jesus' love goes beyond denomination or a set of religious beliefs.

With Miguel I had also experienced once again the joy of a new Christian. When people experience something they have missed or something new, they have so much joy in their heart that they want to share it with their friends and family and neighbors. Jesus told us that we needed to share the Good News with other people. Miguel is a classic example of someone who felt a new sense of joy and release in this life and wanted to share it. He had realized an inner peace and he knew where he was going. Those whom he cared for, his family and friends, did not know the Lord, and Miguel wanted to make sure they experienced His peace and were going to the place where he was going. That should be our mission, to reach out to everybody—our family, friends, neighbors, whomever we meet. If we truly love them, we should be concerned about where they will spend eternity.

My meeting with the Afghan woman had shown me that both of us could share a communion based on a love of God and a plea for His compassionate care for us and our loved ones. I had also had a glimpse into the life of an immigrant who had not been as lucky as I had been in coming to America. She did not speak English well or have a high degree of education. For all I know she did not even have a valid visa to work in the United States. It made me realize that too often we overlook the lives of the immigrants who work in the restaurants, hotels, and other service industries in America. We forget the struggles they go through because they are new to this country and do not have the resources we have. Many of them, like this Afghan woman, are carrying enormous burdens of loss with them that we gloss over in our hurry to get from one place to another. By letting my pen slip out of my pocket, God was telling me that day in the hotel to make sure that I continued to pay attention to the poorest among us, to address their suffering, and to work to bring grace into their lives. God was making sure that I—and by extension all Christians— acknowledged the individual suffering of all peoples, whether they professed Christianity or not, and to value their story, no matter who they were or where they were from.

So this is the first challenge of the Christian life: to give what we have willingly, and be satisfied with the abundance of a rich spiritual life, just as the fisherfolk of Orissa were. For those of us who have plenty of material possessions and do not worry about food supplies or housing, when we realize that God has blessed us with so much, we should not quibble over how much money we have or how difficult life is. In the United States and the developed world, everything is available in an instant: instant money, instant marriage, instant everything. But it not like that in other parts of the world. We need always to keep things in perspective and remember how fortunate we are.

You may be discouraged in your speaking out for God; you may be disappointed by other people's responses. You may wonder why change is not happening as quickly as you had hoped. My response to such discouragement is to remind you that God's timing is something we will never understand. But if we keep pressing on and praying, one day God will open the door and He will honor our love and our cry to be used in the Kingdom of God. He answered my question more immediately than I could possibly have imagined that morning of September 11, when I wrote to my friend worrying about my purpose in life. To those of you who feel useless, who feel you don't have any talents or are not qualified, I say, God wants to use you. He wants to use you in the Kingdom of God, to stand in the gap for your family, neighborhood, and community. God is calling you to be prayer warriors for your churches and the country. Many of you who commit yourselves to God will be called to be evangelists, often on a one-to-one level. Christians have been called by God in places of work and in schools, in different countries and in different professions, to live a Christ-like life, so that through our life and living we can point many to the Cross.

This is my challenge. Go out into your communities. You might be the only people carrying a Bible or speaking about God's love. But press on and there will be others who will join you, because they will want to share in your joy and like you get that ticket to eternity. Remember: One day we will have to give an account for our time on this earth and the opportunities we had. Many of those we love will go without the Gospel if we don't reach out to them.

A Challenge to the Old and the Young

I want to challenge those people who once had a relationship with Jesus Christ but for whatever reason—relationships, life crises, perhaps dislike of the church denomination they belonged to—drifted away from God. I want you to return to your relationship with Jesus and reinvite Him into your heart. I want you to remember just why it was that you felt pulled toward Him. I want that flame to be reignited in your soul. I know in my heart that there were people in the World Trade Center and the Pentagon, and on those planes, who had at some point in their lives heard the message of Jesus Christ. They had responded to that Good News and had understood the great gift that was offered to them. But over the years they had deflected the call because they were busy with their careers, family, and all the other aspects of making our way in this world. As I discovered on September 11, we cannot delay the crucial decision of eternity. All of us need to let Jesus into our heart and hold fast to Him, just as He never stops looking out for us.

I also wish to direct a challenge especially to young people. I am glad to say that in many of my speaking engagements I come across young people who want to be used by God. They tell me they want to go to countries like India and do missionary work, and want to know how they can go about it. When I hear these stories it gladdens my heart because I can see that God has opened doors for them. To those young people who feel called but feel worried that Christianity is boring, I say the enemy is trying to sell you a lie. Christianity is not boring; it is a life of joy in Him. God has always used young people to revive the Christian community, and I believe that young people in the United States have a great role to play, because if they are touched, a generation is touched for the Lord. So I challenge you to live a more consecrated life, devote your love to the Lord, think about His goodness, and have a heart to be used in the Kingdom of God.

If my people, who are called by my name, will humble themselves and pray and seek my face and turn from their wicked ways, then will I hear from heaven and will forgive their sin and will heal their land. (2 Chronicles 7:14)

Conclusion
Beyond Ground Zero

I LEARNED MANY things on September 11. I learned how much I love my wife, and how the possibility of losing her made me do things—such as stopping off to make a phone call on the fifty-third floor of the World Trade Center, or exiting from the south tower rather than the north—that in retrospect seem reckless. It made me realize that at times human beings are amazingly resilient and purposeful, that they have great courage and strength of will. I take daily inspiration from the firefighters and other emergency personnel who ascended to their certain deaths as we descended the stairwell, and from the FBI agent who went back to rescue more people. They have taught me what it means to love selflessly. I learned that there is a great generosity in the human soul, as shown by my coworkers who helped me down the stairs when I was emotionally falling apart, and also opportunism and insensitivity, as shown by the reporter who was more concerned about landing a story than responding to suffering. I learned that God's love, in spite of all our attempts to deny it, never abandons us.

Since September 11, there are two verses from the Bible that have stood out for me, with themes that I have discussed throughout the previous three chapters of this book. The first stands out partly because it is found on page 911 of my Bible. It is from John 4:1–4: "Do not let your hearts be troubled. Trust in God; trust also in me. In my Father's house are many rooms; if it were not so, I would have told you. I am going there to prepare a place for you. And if I go and prepare a place for you, I will come back and take you to be with me that you also may be where I am. You know the way to the place where I am going." Verse 6 continues the theme: "Jesus answered, I am the way and the truth and the life. No one comes to the Father except through me." The other verse that encapsulates my thinking is Acts 4:12: "Salvation is found in no one else, for there is no other name under heaven given to men by which we must be saved."

These are the simple truths that this book has tried to present. It does not matter who you are or what church you belong to; it does not matter what ethnicity or nation you come from. I rejoice in the prospect of arriving in heaven to see millions of people of all times, nations, colors, races, and ethnicities. Though we are divided, we are one in Him (see Romans 14:11). These saints, including the dead of September 11 who gave themselves to Christ, have gone before us. One day, we will die; one day, every denomination and nation-state will fail. However, one name will stand forever, and that is the name of Jesus Christ.

This book has tried to emphasize that because death is certain we had better prepare to answer the question of where we will end up after death: Do you know where you are going? I had prepared for my life by taking out life insurance. But there was a greater insurance for a longer life that I had also taken out—the free gift of the salvation of Jesus Christ. This book, however, can only go so far in addressing the question of where you are going. That question is one that only you can answer, and only you will know the honesty with which you ask it and the honesty with which you attempt an answer. What are your thoughts on eternity? What is your relationship with Jesus Christ? *Do you know where you are going?*

For me, and for millions of others around the world, the answer to the question has been in the joyful acceptance of Jesus Christ into our hearts. Jesus Christ never abandoned me that day—even though I, in all my human frailty, felt angry and wretched. I never lost faith in His saving grace, never lost faith that somehow He had a mission for me, even when immediately before the attack I had been wondering, as a child in Calcutta and even on the very morning of the attack, just what that was. He has kept me steadfast during the months since September 11 as I have traveled around North America with the message of the Good News. He has made sure that I do not forget those who are suffering, like the Afghan woman, even as I spend time with those who are blessed with material possessions. His presence is a daily joy and a daily challenge amid the trials and tribulations of being a professing Christian in the twenty-first century. He is truly, like my church in Calcutta, a lighthouse of hope.

This book has attempted to show that at each point of my life, when things seemed their bleakest, God's will was working in the world. It was working to call upon all His people to turn to Him and buy their ticket to eternity through an invitation to let Him enter their heart. I invite and urge you to do the same.

On September 11, over two thousand people died at the World Trade Center, a site that, within a few hours, had come to be called Ground Zero. As I write, that site has now been cleared of the millions of tons of debris in preparation for whatever rebuilding will take place there and the plans have been drafted. Yet that site always will be, in some way, holy ground.

I like to think of Ground Zero, however, in a broader sense. As a Christian who professes the name of Jesus Christ, for me Ground Zero has other meanings than the shattered remnants of a vibrant community of souls in lower Manhattan with whom I had the privilege of working and sharing space for a few months. Ground Zero is all of our places of work. It is our community, our neighborhoods, everywhere where God takes us, where people are perishing forever without Jesus Christ, and where we can make a difference by asking people if they know where they are going and offering them the opportunity of knowing Jesus Christ.

Ground Zero is the place of hope that comes out of the ashes. It is a place of restoration, where in our own failure God takes over and gives us the hope and strength to carry on. In the days immediately after September 11, no one had the answers or knew what the future was. Yet God held this country together and made us stronger than ever.

Ground Zero in Manhattan is the place where our dreams crashed to the ground. Ground Zero in our hearts is the place where we can build our lives afresh, joyfully anointed by the Holy Spirit and the saving grace of Jesus Christ, blessed with a new sense of commitment and hope in Him, and looking forward with joyful expectation to the promise that we will join all those who have gone before us in eternal life.

Epilogue ❧
Jeremy's Birth

MARCH 2, 2002, was one of the most thrilling days in our lives. Our son, Jeremy David John, was born a healthy baby nearly seven pounds in weight at Pascack Valley Hospital, New Jersey.

The day I learned that Mary was pregnant I was ecstatic. She will tell you that I was jumping around the house unable to contain my joy! During her pregnancy, Mary often asked me to pick out a name for our child, but I would hesitate, saying there was still time. Like many expectant parents, Mary and I counted the days to the arrival of our child, and there were many nights when Mary would let me feel the movements of the baby she was carrying.

Then on September 11 there were the interminable hours when I thought that Mary and the child she was carrying was dead, while Mary was likewise thinking that her child would never see its father. My first thought on seeing Mary was "I hope the baby is doing fine." I remember all too well those anxious moments when we finally arrived home that night and tried to hear the baby's heartbeat. I took Mary to her doctor, who told us that the baby was fine and there was nothing to worry about. While our fears were ended, deep within I knew that if God had saved both of us, He had a plan for our baby as well.

We did not have to go through too many names before deciding one. We decided to name him Jeremy, after Jeremiah, which means "Appointed by God." We know for sure that God has appointed Him for a task and that when he grows up he will be a witness of His grace and love. Every time I travel with Jeremy, people tell us that he is sign of God's protection and grace.

Jeremy has brought so much joy into our lives. It is hard for me to leave him on those days when I travel to share my message. There are times when I see him smile and I just cannot help but cry, because I am reminded of God's mercy and faithfulness and of how He spared my life and allowed me to enjoy these beautiful moments of seeing my son grow.

There have, however, been moments when I have asked myself this question: Into what world has my son arrived? Our world has changed so much since September 11. It is incumbent upon us to work toward peace through the world. My heart also goes out to the hundreds if not thousands of children who lost their parents on September 11. My heart breaks for the many babies who have come into this world since that fateful day and will never experience the warmth and love of an earthly father. But one thing I know: God is watching over these little ones. He is a father to the fatherless and a mother to the motherless.

What we need to remember always is that if we as earthly parents care so much for our children, how much more does our Heavenly Father care for us? Our Eternal Father longs to embrace us with His love; there is no measure to the love He pours into our life.

For God so loved the world that He gave His one and only Son, that whoever believes in Him shall not perish but have eternal life (2 Chronicles 7:14).

Appendix ❧
The Sinner's Prayer
and the Prayer of Jabez

I KNOW IN my heart that God has been speaking to your heart even we you were reading this book. He is asking you to make a decision for Him. He is inviting you to begin living an exciting personal relationship with Him.

The amazing thing is that you do not have to wait any longer. This is your appointed time. Wherever you are at this moment, you are not far from Him. If you have realized that you are a sinner and that Jesus is the only way to salvation, you are on the pathway to real freedom in Christ.

Would you begin this exciting journey by saying this prayer in your heart?

Dear Jesus,
Thank you for speaking to my heart. Lord Jesus, I am a sinner. I am sorry for my sins and for all the times that I have grieved Your heart. You took my place on the cruel cross, You died for my sins and by Your blood I can have forgiveness for my sins. I receive You as my Savior. Lord, I thank You for eternal life, which You have promised for them that call upon Your name. I thank Jesus for Your unconditional love.
In Jesus' name,
Amen.

If you have said that prayer: Congratulations! You have made the most important decision of your life. May God bless you and your new relationship with Jesus. Welcome to the family of God. I would love to hear from you about the life-transforming experience that you have had in saying this prayer. Remember, this is just the start of many exciting things that will happen in your life. You can reach me at: sujo@sujojohn.com.

The Prayer of Jabez
God is inviting each one of us to be an "overcomer." Each one of us has been created in His likeness for a unique purpose. When was the last time you wept before the Lord asking God to bless you? The Bible says, "Ask and it will be given to you; seek and you will find; knock and the door will be opened to you" (Matthew 7:7). Your difficult circumstances are not hidden from God. He is the God that creates streams in the desert. His plans for us are to prosper and be blessed.

I started saying the Prayer of Jabez a couple of days before September 11, 2001, and this powerful prayer has changed my life. This prayer is powerful because you are inviting God to take the foremost position in your work, in your family life, and in all that you do. The prayer is offered by Jabez, one of the sons of Judah, in the First Book of Chronicles (4:9–10) in the Old Testament.

I invite you to pray with me the powerful words that Jabez prayed:

Oh, that You would bless me indeed, and enlarge my territory, that Your hand would be with me, and that You would keep me from evil, that I may not cause pain!

Mission of Mercy 🌸

I have shared throughout this book the work being carried on by my home church in Calcutta, India. Millions of hurting people are being reached by the generosity of many people like you. The greatest investment you can make in your lifetime is to invest in people. If you want to partner Mission of Mercy in their work in India, or find out more about them, please get in touch with them at the following addresses:

Mission of Mercy
P.O. Box 62600
Colorado Springs, CO 80962

or

Mission of Mercy
15475 Gleneagle Drive
Colorado Springs, CO 80921
Tel.: (719) 481-0400
Fax: (719) 481-4649
www.missionofmercy.org